HEALTHY HEART DIET: LOW CHOLESTE[ROL RECIPES] TO KEEP YOUR HEART HAPPY

First edition. March 18, 2024.

ISBN: 979-8224970247

Written by Gupta Amit.

Table of Contents

Healthy Heart Diet: Low Cholesterol Meals To Keep Your Heart Happy

Lemon garlic shrimp skewers

Ingredients:

- 1 lb shrimp
- 2 lemons
- 4 cloves garlic
- 2 tbsp olive oil
- Salt and pepper

Equipment:

1. Grill
2. Skewers
3. Tongs
4. Bowls
5. Whisk
6. Knife

Methods:

Step 1: Soak wooden skewers in water for 30 minutes.

Step 2: In a mixing bowl, combine 1/4 cup olive oil, 3 cloves minced garlic, 1 tablespoon lemon juice, 1 teaspoon lemon zest, 1/2 teaspoon salt, and 1/4 teaspoon black pepper.

Step 3: Add 1 pound peeled and deveined shrimp to the marinade and toss to coat.

Step 4: Thread shrimp onto skewers, making sure to leave space between each shrimp.

Step 5: Preheat grill to medium-high heat.

Step 6: Grill shrimp skewers for 2-3 minutes per side or until shrimp is pink and opaque.

Step 7: Serve hot and enjoy!

Helpful Tips:

1. Marinate the shrimp in a mixture of lemon juice, minced garlic, olive oil, salt, and pepper for at least 30 minutes before skewering.

2. Use metal or wooden skewers that have been soaked in water for at least 30 minutes to prevent burning.

3. Alternate the shrimp with slices of lemon and fresh herbs like parsley or basil for added flavor.

4. Preheat your grill or broiler to high heat before cooking the skewers.

5. Cook the shrimp skewers for 2-3 minutes on each side, or until they are opaque and cooked through.

6. Serve the skewers with extra lemon wedges for squeezing over the top before serving.

Turkey meatloaf with oats and vegetables

Ingredients:

- 1 lb ground turkey
- 1 cup rolled oats
- 1/2 cup diced onion
- 1/2 cup diced bell pepper
- 1/2 cup grated carrot
- 2 cloves minced garlic
- 1/4 cup ketchup
- 1 egg
- 1 tsp salt
- 1/2 tsp pepper

Equipment:

1. Mixing bowl
2. Cutting board
3. Knife
4. Baking dish
5. Wooden spoon

Methods:

Step 1: Preheat the oven to 350°F.

Step 2: In a bowl, mix together 1 lb ground turkey, 1 cup oats, 1/2 cup chopped bell peppers, 1/2 cup chopped onion, 1/4 cup shredded carrots, 2 cloves minced garlic, 1/4 cup ketchup, 1 beaten egg, 1 tsp salt, and 1/2 tsp pepper.

Step 3: Shape the mixture into a loaf and place it in a greased loaf pan.

Step 4: Bake the meatloaf in the preheated oven for 45-50 minutes, or until cooked through.

Step 5: Let the meatloaf rest for 10 minutes before slicing and serving. Enjoy your delicious turkey meatloaf with oats and vegetables!

Helpful Tips:

1. Preheat your oven to 350°F.

2. Use lean ground turkey meat to keep the meatloaf healthy.

3. Incorporate oats into the mixture for added fiber and texture.

4. Use a variety of finely chopped vegetables such as onions, bell peppers, and carrots for added flavor and nutrients.

5. Season the meatloaf with your favorite herbs and spices for a delicious taste.

6. Mix all ingredients together thoroughly but avoid overmixing to keep the meatloaf tender.

7. Shape the mixture into a loaf shape and place it in a greased loaf pan.

8. Bake for about 45-50 minutes or until the internal temperature reaches 165°F.

9. Let the meatloaf rest for a few minutes before slicing and serving. Enjoy!

Eggplant Parmesan with whole wheat breadcrumbs

Ingredients:
- 2 large eggplants
- 1 cup whole wheat breadcrumbs
- 1 cup marinara sauce
- 2 cups shredded mozzarella cheese

Equipment:
1. Baking dish
2. Mixing bowl
3. Whisk
4. Chef's knife
5. Cutting board

Methods:
Step 1: Preheat the oven to 375°F and grease a baking dish with olive oil.

Step 2: Slice the eggplant into 1/2 inch rounds and sprinkle with salt. Let sit for 15 minutes to draw out moisture.

Step 3: Rinse the eggplant, pat dry, and dip each round into flour, then egg, and finally whole wheat breadcrumbs.

Step 4: Place the breaded eggplant rounds on the greased baking dish and bake for 25 minutes.

Step 5: Remove from the oven and top each round with marinara sauce and shredded mozzarella cheese.

Step 6: Return to the oven and bake for an additional 15 minutes or until cheese is melted and bubbly.

Step 7: Serve hot and enjoy your Eggplant Parmesan with whole wheat breadcrumbs.

Helpful Tips:
1. Use whole wheat breadcrumbs for a healthier twist on this classic dish.
2. Slice the eggplant thinly and evenly for even cooking.

3. Salt the eggplant slices and let them sit for 30 minutes to remove excess moisture and bitterness.

4. Dip the eggplant slices in beaten egg before coating them in breadcrumbs to help the coating adhere.

5. Bake the eggplant slices instead of frying them for a lighter version of Eggplant Parmesan.

6. Layer the baked eggplant slices with marinara sauce and mozzarella cheese for maximum flavor.

7. Top with grated Parmesan cheese before serving for an extra cheesy kick.

Mediterranean vegetable and bean stew

Ingredients:

- 1 onion
- 2 cloves of garlic
- 1 red pepper
- 1 zucchini
- 1 can of diced tomatoes
- 1 can of cannellini beans
- 1 tsp dried oregano
- 1 tsp dried basil
- Salt and pepper to taste

Equipment:

1. Dutch oven
2. Chef's knife
3. Cutting board
4. Wooden spoon
5. Saucepan

Methods:

Step 1: Heat olive oil in a large pot over medium heat.

Step 2: Add diced onions and minced garlic, cook until onions are translucent.

Step 3: Stir in diced bell peppers, zucchini, and eggplant.

Step 4: Add diced tomatoes, tomato sauce, vegetable broth, and a bay leaf.

Step 5: Season with salt, pepper, dried oregano, and dried basil.

Step 6: Stir in drained and rinsed cannellini beans and chickpeas.

Step 7: Cover and let simmer for 20-25 minutes.

Step 8: Serve hot, garnished with fresh parsley and a drizzle of olive oil. Enjoy your Mediterranean vegetable and bean stew!

Helpful Tips:

1. Start by sautéing onions and garlic in olive oil for extra flavor.

2. Add a variety of Mediterranean vegetables such as eggplant, zucchini, tomatoes, and bell peppers for a colorful and nutritious stew.

3. Use dried herbs like oregano, thyme, and rosemary for an authentic Mediterranean flavor.

4. Add canned beans such as chickpeas or cannellini beans for protein and texture.

5. Consider adding some chopped olives or capers for an extra burst of flavor.

6. Simmer the stew on low heat to allow the flavors to meld together.

7. Serve the stew with crusty bread or over couscous for a hearty meal.

Roasted beet salad with walnuts and goat cheese

Ingredients:

- 4 beets
- 1/4 cup walnuts
- 2 oz goat cheese
- 4 cups mixed greens

Equipment:

1. Knife
2. Cutting board
3. Mixing bowl
4. Whisk
5. Salad tongs

Methods:

Step 1: Preheat oven to 400°F.

Step 2: Scrub beets and trim off the tops and roots.

Step 3: Wrap beets individually in foil and place on a baking sheet.

Step 4: Roast beets in the oven for 45-60 minutes, or until tender.

Step 5: Let beets cool, then peel and dice them.

Step 6: Toast walnuts on a dry skillet until fragrant.

Step 7: In a large bowl, mix arugula, roasted beets, toasted walnuts, and crumbled goat cheese.

Step 8: Drizzle with balsamic vinaigrette and toss to combine.

Step 9: Serve the roasted beet salad immediately and enjoy!

Helpful Tips:

1. Start by roasting the beets in the oven at 400°F for about 45 minutes or until they are tender.

2. While the beets are roasting, toast the walnuts in a dry skillet over medium heat until fragrant.

3. Once the beets are done, allow them to cool slightly before peeling and slicing them.

4. Arrange the beets on a bed of greens, such as arugula or mixed baby greens.

5. Crumble the goat cheese over the top of the salad.

6. Drizzle with a vinaigrette made from olive oil, balsamic vinegar, and a hint of honey.

7. Sprinkle the toasted walnuts over the top for added crunch.

8. Serve immediately and enjoy your delicious roasted beet salad!

Broccoli and cheddar quiche with whole wheat crust

Ingredients:

- 1 cup whole wheat flour
- 1/2 cup olive oil
- 1 small head of broccoli
- 1 cup shredded cheddar cheese
- 4 eggs
- 1 cup milk
- Salt and pepper to taste

Equipment:

1. Mixing bowl
2. Whisk
3. Pie dish
4. Rolling pin
5. Knife

Methods:

Step 1: Preheat the oven to 375°F and grease a 9-inch pie dish.

Step 2: In a mixing bowl, combine 1 cup of whole wheat flour, 1/4 cup of melted butter, and a pinch of salt. Mix until a dough forms.

Step 3: Press the dough into the greased pie dish, making sure to cover the bottom and sides evenly.

Step 4: In a separate bowl, whisk together 4 eggs, 1 cup of milk, salt, and pepper.

Step 5: Stir in 1 cup of shredded cheddar cheese and chopped broccoli florets.

Step 6: Pour the egg mixture into the prepared crust.

Step 7: Bake for 35-40 minutes, or until the quiche is set and the crust is golden brown.

Step 8: Let it cool for a few minutes before slicing and serving. Enjoy your broccoli and cheddar quiche with whole wheat crust!

Helpful Tips:

1. Preheat your oven to 375°F and prepare a pie dish or tart pan with whole wheat crust.

2. Steam or blanch the broccoli florets until they are slightly tender, then chop into small pieces.

3. Whisk together eggs, milk, shredded cheddar cheese, salt, and pepper in a bowl until well combined.

4. Add the chopped broccoli to the egg mixture and pour into the prepared crust.

5. Bake for 30-35 minutes or until the quiche is set and the crust is golden brown.

6. Let the quiche cool slightly before slicing and serving for best results.

Lemon herb roasted chicken thighs

Ingredients:

- 8 bone-in, skin-on chicken thighs
- 2 lemons, juiced and zested
- 2 tbsp olive oil
- 2 cloves of garlic, minced
- 1 tbsp fresh rosemary, chopped
- 1 tbsp fresh thyme, chopped
- Salt and pepper to taste

Equipment:

1. Mixing bowl
2. Baking sheet
3. Tongs
4. Kitchen knife
5. Oven mitts

Methods:

Step 1: Preheat the oven to 425°F (220°C).

Step 2: In a small bowl, combine chopped fresh herbs (such as rosemary, thyme, and parsley), minced garlic, lemon zest, and olive oil.

Step 3: Place chicken thighs in a baking dish and season with salt and pepper.

Step 4: Rub the herb mixture onto the chicken thighs, making sure they are evenly coated.

Step 5: Squeeze lemon juice over the chicken and add lemon slices to the baking dish.

Step 6: Roast in the oven for 25-30 minutes, or until the chicken is cooked through and the skin is crispy.

Step 7: Serve hot and enjoy your lemon herb roasted chicken thighs.

Helpful Tips:

1. Preheat oven to 400 degrees F.

2. In a small bowl, mix together olive oil, lemon juice, minced garlic, salt, pepper, and chopped herbs (such as rosemary, thyme, and parsley).

3. Place chicken thighs in a baking dish and pour the marinade over them.

4. Rub the marinade into the chicken thighs, ensuring they are evenly coated.

5. Cover the baking dish with foil and let the chicken marinate in the fridge for at least 30 minutes.

6. Remove foil and bake chicken thighs for 25-30 minutes, or until juices run clear and internal temperature reaches 165 degrees F.

7. Serve hot with your favorite sides. Enjoy!

Low-fat turkey and vegetable lasagna

Ingredients:

- 9 whole wheat lasagna noodles
- 1 lb ground turkey
- 1 onion, chopped
- 2 cloves garlic, minced
- 1 bell pepper, chopped
- 1 zucchini, chopped
- 1 cup marinara sauce
- 1 cup low-fat ricotta cheese
- 1 cup low-fat mozzarella cheese
- 1/4 cup grated Parmesan cheese

Equipment:

1. Knife
2. Cutting board
3. Mixing bowl
4. Saucepan
5. Baking dish

Methods:

Step 1: Preheat the oven to 375°F.

Step 2: In a skillet, cook lean ground turkey until browned. Add chopped onion, garlic, and bell pepper. Cook until vegetables are soft.

Step 3: Stir in diced tomatoes, tomato sauce, Italian seasoning, salt, and pepper.

Step 4: In a separate bowl, mix low-fat ricotta cheese, egg whites, and grated Parmesan cheese.

Step 5: Spread a layer of the turkey mixture on the bottom of a baking dish.

Step 6: Layer lasagna noodles, turkey mixture, ricotta mixture, and shredded reduced-fat mozzarella cheese.

Step 7: Repeat layers, ending with a layer of mozzarella cheese.

Step 8: Cover with foil and bake for 30 minutes. Remove foil and bake for an additional 15 minutes. Enjoy!

Helpful Tips:

1. Use lean ground turkey instead of beef for a lower fat option.

2. Add plenty of vegetables like bell peppers, zucchini, and spinach for added nutrients.

3. Use whole wheat or gluten-free lasagna noodles for a healthier alternative.

4. Opt for low-fat or part-skim mozzarella cheese to cut down on saturated fat.

5. Make a homemade marinara sauce with fresh tomatoes, garlic, and herbs for a lower sodium option.

6. Layer the lasagna with a thin layer of cheese and incorporate more vegetables to reduce calories.

7. Bake the lasagna uncovered to allow excess moisture to evaporate, resulting in a firmer consistency.

8. Let the lasagna sit for a few minutes before serving to allow it to set and make for easier slicing.

Spicy black bean soup with avocado

Ingredients:

- 2 cans black beans
- 1 cup vegetable broth
- 1 onion, chopped
- 2 cloves garlic, minced
- 1 tsp cumin
- 1 tsp chili powder
- 1/2 avocado, diced
- 1 lime, juiced

Equipment:

1. Saucepan
2. Wooden spoon
3. Ladle
4. Blender
5. Cutting board
6. Knife

Methods:

Step 1: Heat olive oil in a large pot over medium heat.

Step 2: Add chopped onions, garlic, and jalapenos to the pot and sauté until softened.

Step 3: Stir in black beans, diced tomatoes, vegetable broth, cumin, chili powder, and salt.

Step 4: Bring the mixture to a boil, then reduce heat and let simmer for 15 minutes.

Step 5: Remove the pot from heat and use an immersion blender to partially blend the soup, leaving some chunks of beans.

Step 6: Serve the soup hot, topped with diced avocado, fresh cilantro, and a squeeze of lime juice. Enjoy!

Helpful Tips:

1. Start by sautéing onions and garlic in olive oil until they are soft.

2. Add in your spices such as cumin, chili powder, and paprika to give the soup a flavorful kick.

3. Stir in black beans, vegetable broth, and diced tomatoes, then bring the mixture to a simmer.

4. Carefully blend the soup with an immersion blender until smooth.

5. Add diced avocado right before serving for a creamy and nutritious addition.

6. Garnish with fresh cilantro, a dollop of sour cream, and a squeeze of lime juice for an extra burst of flavor.

7. Serve with crusty bread or tortilla chips for dipping.

Baked pesto salmon

Ingredients:

- 4 salmon fillets
- 4 tbsp pesto
- 2 tbsp olive oil
- 1 lemon
- Salt and pepper
- Fresh basil for garnish
- 135 letters long

Equipment:

1. Baking dish
2. Mixing bowl
3. Whisk
4. Spatula
5. Aluminum foil
6. Oven mitts

Methods:

Step 1: Preheat the oven to 375°F.

Step 2: Place a salmon fillet on a baking sheet lined with parchment paper.

Step 3: Spread a generous amount of pesto sauce over the top of the salmon.

Step 4: Drizzle some olive oil over the pesto.

Step 5: Season with salt and pepper.

Step 6: Place the baking sheet in the preheated oven.

Step 7: Bake for 15-20 minutes, or until the salmon is cooked through and flakes easily with a fork.

Step 8: Remove from the oven and let it rest for a few minutes before serving.

Step 9: Enjoy your delicious baked pesto salmon!

Helpful Tips:

1. Preheat the oven to 400°F and line a baking sheet with parchment paper.

2. Place salmon fillets on the prepared baking sheet and season with salt and pepper.

3. Spread a generous amount of pesto sauce over the top of each fillet.

4. Add slices of lemon on top for extra flavor.

5. Bake in the preheated oven for 12-15 minutes, or until the salmon is cooked through and flakes easily with a fork.

6. Serve hot with your favorite side dishes, such as roasted vegetables or a salad.

7. Enjoy the delicious and healthy baked pesto salmon!

Grilled swordfish with lemon and capers

Ingredients:

- 4 swordfish fillets
- Juice of 1 lemon
- 2 tbsp capers
- Salt and pepper to taste

Equipment:

1. Grilling pan
2. Lemon squeezer
3. Tongs
4. Serving platter
5. Knife
6. Cutting board

Methods:

Step 1: Preheat grill to medium-high heat.

Step 2: Season swordfish steaks with salt and pepper.

Step 3: Brush swordfish with olive oil.

Step 4: Place swordfish on the grill and cook for 4-5 minutes per side, or until it reaches an internal temperature of 145°F.

Step 5: In a small saucepan, melt butter and add capers, lemon juice, and minced garlic.

Step 6: Cook for 2-3 minutes until the sauce thickens slightly.

Step 7: Remove swordfish from the grill and top with the lemon caper sauce.

Step 8: Serve the grilled swordfish with lemon wedges and fresh herbs. Enjoy!

Helpful Tips:

1. Start by marinating the swordfish in a mixture of lemon juice, olive oil, salt, pepper, and minced garlic for at least 30 minutes.

2. Preheat your grill to medium-high heat and brush the grates with oil to prevent sticking.

3. Grill the swordfish for about 4-5 minutes per side, or until it reaches an internal temperature of 145°F.

4. While the swordfish is grilling, prepare a sauce by combining melted butter, capers, lemon zest, and chopped parsley.

5. Serve the grilled swordfish topped with the lemon caper sauce and enjoy with your favorite side dishes.

Tofu and vegetable coconut curry

Ingredients:
- 1 block of tofu
- 1 cup of mixed vegetables
- 1 can of coconut milk
- 2 tbsp curry paste
- 1 tbsp soy sauce
- 1 tsp ginger

Equipment:
1. Saucepan
2. Wooden spoon
3. Chef's knife
4. Cutting board
5. Ladle

Methods:
Step 1: Heat a large pan over medium heat and add a tablespoon of oil.

Step 2: Add diced onion and cook until soft, about 5 minutes.

Step 3: Stir in curry paste and cook for another minute.

Step 4: Add diced tofu and vegetables of your choice (bell peppers, broccoli, carrots).

Step 5: Pour in a can of coconut milk and bring to a simmer.

Step 6: Let simmer for 15-20 minutes, until vegetables are tender.

Step 7: Season with salt and pepper to taste.

Step 8: Serve over rice or noodles and enjoy your delicious tofu and vegetable coconut curry!

Helpful Tips:
1. Use extra-firm tofu to prevent it from falling apart during cooking.

2. Press tofu before cooking to remove excess moisture and improve the texture.

3. Cut tofu into cubes or triangles for better absorption of flavors.

4. Opt for a variety of colorful vegetables like bell peppers, carrots, and broccoli for added nutrition.

5. Consider adding vegetables with varying textures to create a more interesting dish.

6. Use full-fat coconut milk for a creamier curry or light coconut milk for a lighter option.

7. Toast spices like cumin, coriander, and turmeric before adding them to enhance their flavor.

8. Garnish with fresh herbs like cilantro or basil for a burst of freshness.

Spinach and lentil dal

Ingredients:

- 1 cup red lentils
- 4 cups baby spinach
- 1 onion, diced
- 2 cloves garlic, minced
- 1 tsp cumin
- 1 tsp turmeric
- 4 cups vegetable broth

Equipment:

1. Ladle
2. Wooden spoon
3. Spatula
4. Whisk
5. Tongs

Methods:

Step 1: Rinse 1 cup of lentils and soak them in water for 30 minutes.

Step 2: In a large pot, heat 2 tablespoons of oil and add 1 chopped onion, 3 minced garlic cloves, and 1 tablespoon of grated ginger.

Step 3: Cook until the onion is soft and translucent.

Step 4: Add 1 teaspoon of cumin, 1 teaspoon of coriander, and 1/2 teaspoon of turmeric.

Step 5: Stir in the soaked lentils, 4 cups of vegetable broth, and 2 cups of chopped spinach.

Step 6: Simmer for 30 minutes or until the lentils are tender.

Step 7: Season with salt and pepper to taste before serving.

Helpful Tips:

1. Wash lentils thoroughly before cooking to remove any dirt or debris.

2. Use a ratio of 1 part lentils to 3 parts water for cooking.

3. Add chopped spinach towards the end of cooking to retain its vibrant green color.

4. Season generously with a mix of spices like cumin, coriander, turmeric, and garam masala.

5. For added flavor, sizzle mustard seeds, cumin seeds, and curry leaves in hot oil before adding to the dal.

6. Finish with a splash of fresh lemon juice for a bright and tangy flavor.

7. Serve hot with rice or naan bread for a complete meal.

Turkey and vegetable stuffed bell peppers

Ingredients:
- 4 bell peppers
- 1 lb ground turkey
- 1 cup cooked quinoa
- 1 cup diced tomatoes
- 1/2 cup diced onion
- 1/2 cup shredded cheese

Equipment:
1. Large knife
2. Cutting board
3. Skillet
4. Mixing bowl
5. Spoon
6. Oven dish

Methods:
Step 1: Preheat the oven to 375°F.

Step 2: Cut off the tops of the bell peppers and remove the seeds and membranes.

Step 3: In a skillet, cook ground turkey until browned.

Step 4: Add diced onions, garlic, and your choice of mixed vegetables to the skillet and cook until softened.

Step 5: Stir in cooked quinoa, diced tomatoes, and spices such as salt, pepper, and Italian seasoning.

Step 6: Stuff the bell peppers with the turkey and vegetable mixture.

Step 7: Place the stuffed bell peppers in a baking dish and cover with foil.

Step 8: Bake for 25-30 minutes or until the peppers are tender. Enjoy your turkey and vegetable stuffed bell peppers!

Helpful Tips:
1. Preheat your oven to 375°F before starting the recipe.
2. Use a mix of ground turkey and vegetables for a healthier stuffing option.

3. Cut the bell peppers in half vertically to make it easier to stuff.

4. Remove the seeds and membrane from the inside of the bell peppers before filling them.

5. Season the turkey and vegetable mixture well with herbs and spices for added flavor.

6. Top the stuffed bell peppers with cheese before baking for a delicious cheesy finish.

7. Cover the baking dish with foil to trap in moisture and cook the peppers evenly.

8. Bake for 25-30 minutes or until the peppers are tender and the filling is cooked through.

9. Serve hot and enjoy your delicious turkey and vegetable stuffed bell peppers!

Ratatouille with whole grain couscous

Ingredients:

- 1 eggplant (cubed)
- 2 zucchinis (sliced)
- 1 red bell pepper (sliced)
- 1 yellow onion (chopped)
- 2 cloves of garlic (minced)
- 1 can of diced tomatoes
- 1 tsp dried basil
- 1 tsp dried oregano
- 1 cup of whole grain couscous

Equipment:

1. Cutting board
2. Chef's knife
3. Skillet
4. Wooden spoon
5. Pot
6. Mixing bowls

Methods:

Step 1: Preheat the oven to 400°F.

Step 2: Chop 1 eggplant, 2 zucchinis, 1 bell pepper, and 1 onion into small cubes.

Step 3: Toss the chopped vegetables with olive oil, salt, pepper, and herbs like thyme and rosemary.

Step 4: Spread the vegetables on a baking sheet and roast in the oven for 25-30 minutes.

Step 5: In a saucepan, bring 1 1/2 cups of vegetable broth to a boil.

Step 6: Stir in 1 cup of whole grain couscous, cover, and remove from heat. Let it sit for 5 minutes.

Step 7: Fluff the couscous with a fork and serve with the roasted vegetables on top. Enjoy your ratatouille with whole grain couscous!

Helpful Tips:

1. Start by preparing all your vegetables - bell peppers, eggplant, zucchini, and tomatoes - and chop them into bite-sized pieces.

2. Heat some olive oil in a large skillet or pan over medium heat.

3. Add the vegetables to the skillet, starting with the bell peppers and eggplant as they take longer to cook.

4. Season the vegetables with salt, pepper, and your favorite herbs like thyme or basil.

5. Once the vegetables are cooked through and tender, stir in a can of tomato sauce or diced tomatoes.

6. While the ratatouille simmers, prepare the whole grain couscous according to package instructions.

7. Serve the ratatouille over the couscous and enjoy your healthy and delicious meal.

Beet and chickpea salad with tahini dressing

Ingredients:

- 2 medium beets (sliced)
- 1 can of chickpeas (drained)
- 2 tbsp tahini
- 1 tbsp olive oil
- Salt and pepper to taste

Equipment:

1. Mixing bowl
2. Whisk
3. Measuring spoons
4. Salad tongs
5. Serving dish

Methods:

Step 1: Preheat your oven to 400°F.

Step 2: Peel and dice 2 large beets and toss them in olive oil, salt, and pepper.

Step 3: Roast the beets in the oven for 30-40 minutes or until tender.

Step 4: Drain and rinse a can of chickpeas and toss them with olive oil, cumin, and paprika.

Step 5: Roast the chickpeas in the oven for 20-25 minutes or until crispy.

Step 6: In a small bowl, whisk together 1/4 cup tahini, 2 tablespoons lemon juice, 1 clove of minced garlic, and 2 tablespoons of water.

Step 7: Mix the roasted beets, chickpeas, and tahini dressing together in a bowl.

Step 8: Serve the salad chilled or at room temperature. Enjoy!

Helpful Tips:

1. Begin by roasting the beets in the oven at 400°F for about 45 minutes or until tender.

2. Drain and rinse a can of chickpeas before mixing them with the roasted beets.

3. Prepare the tahini dressing by whisking together tahini, lemon juice, garlic, water, and salt and pepper.

4. Drizzle the tahini dressing over the beet and chickpea mixture and toss well to combine.

5. Top the salad with fresh herbs like parsley or cilantro for added flavor.

6. Serve the salad chilled or at room temperature for best taste.

7. Enjoy as a healthy side dish or as a light meal!

Cauliflower and potato curry

Ingredients:

- 1 head of cauliflower
- 2 large potatoes
- 1 onion
- 2 cloves of garlic
- 1 can of coconut milk
- 2 tbsp curry powder
- Salt and pepper, to taste

Equipment:

1. Chef's knife
2. Cutting board
3. Saucepan
4. Wooden spoon
5. Vegetable peeler

Methods:

Step 1: Wash and chop one medium cauliflower and two large potatoes.

Step 2: Heat oil in a large pan and add one finely chopped onion.

Step 3: Add one teaspoon of cumin seeds, one teaspoon of turmeric, and one tablespoon of curry powder to the pan.

Step 4: Cook until the onions are soft, then add the chopped cauliflower and potatoes.

Step 5: Stir well and cook for 5 minutes.

Step 6: Add one can of diced tomatoes and one cup of vegetable broth.

Step 7: Cover and simmer for 20 minutes, or until the vegetables are tender.

Step 8: Serve hot with rice or naan bread.

Helpful Tips:

1. Begin by washing and chopping the cauliflower into small florets, and peeling and dicing the potatoes.

2. Toast your spices (such as cumin, coriander, turmeric, and chili powder) in a dry pan before adding to the curry for maximum flavor.

3. Use a combination of oil and ghee for frying the onions and garlic to enhance the overall taste of the dish.

4. Add chopped tomatoes or tomato puree for a rich and tangy base to the curry.

5. Opt for coconut milk or yogurt to add creaminess to the dish, balancing out the spices.

6. Garnish with fresh cilantro and a squeeze of lemon juice before serving for a burst of freshness.

BBQ pulled chicken with homemade sauce

Ingredients:
- 1 lb chicken breast
- 1 cup BBQ sauce
- 1/4 cup brown sugar
- 1/4 cup apple cider vinegar
- 1 tsp garlic powder
- 1 tsp paprika
- 1 tsp salt
- 1 tsp pepper

Equipment:
1. Knife
2. Cutting board
3. Saucepan
4. Wooden spoon
5. Tongs

Methods:
Step 1: Season chicken breasts with salt, pepper, and onion powder.

Step 2: Place seasoned chicken breasts on a preheated grill and cook until fully cooked.

Step 3: In a saucepan, combine ketchup, brown sugar, apple cider vinegar, Worcestershire sauce, garlic powder, and mustard.

Step 4: Simmer sauce over low heat until sugar is fully dissolved.

Step 5: Shred the cooked chicken breasts using two forks.

Step 6: Pour the homemade sauce over the shredded chicken and mix well.

Step 7: Serve the BBQ pulled chicken on buns or over rice.

Step 8: Enjoy your delicious homemade BBQ pulled chicken!

Helpful Tips:
1. Start by seasoning your chicken with a dry rub of your choice before cooking it in the slow cooker.

2. Make your own BBQ sauce by combining ketchup, brown sugar, Worcestershire sauce, apple cider vinegar, and spices in a saucepan over low heat.

3. Shred the cooked chicken with two forks and mix in the homemade BBQ sauce.

4. Serve the pulled chicken on toasted buns with coleslaw or pickles for extra flavor.

5. Don't forget to let the flavors meld together for at least 15-20 minutes before serving. Enjoy your delicious BBQ pulled chicken!

Roasted red pepper and goat cheese frittata

Ingredients:

- 8 eggs
- 1/2 cup roasted red peppers
- 1/2 cup crumbled goat cheese
- Salt and pepper

Equipment:

1. Whisk
2. Skillet
3. Spatula
4. Chef's knife
5. Cutting board

Methods:

Step 1: Preheat the oven to 375°F and grease a 9-inch pie dish.

Step 2: Roast 2 red peppers until charred, peel off skin, and chop into strips.

Step 3: In a skillet, sauté 1 diced onion and 2 minced garlic cloves until soft.

Step 4: In a bowl, whisk 8 eggs with 1/4 cup of milk and season with salt and pepper.

Step 5: Pour the egg mixture into the pie dish and add the roasted red peppers, sautéed onions, and 1/2 cup of crumbled goat cheese.

Step 6: Bake in the oven for 25-30 minutes, or until the frittata is set and golden brown. Enjoy!

Helpful Tips:

1. Preheat your oven to 350°F before you start preparing the frittata.

2. Roast red peppers in the oven or on a stovetop flame until they are charred on all sides, then peel and chop them.

3. Beat eggs with salt, pepper, and herbs in a large bowl until well combined.

4. Pour the egg mixture into a greased oven-safe skillet over medium heat.

5. Add the roasted red peppers and crumbled goat cheese to the skillet, stirring gently.

6. Transfer the skillet to the preheated oven and bake for 15-20 minutes, or until the frittata is set and slightly browned on top.

7. Serve the frittata hot or at room temperature, garnished with fresh herbs. Enjoy!

Lentil and vegetable shepherd's pie

Ingredients:

- 2 cups cooked lentils
- 1 onion, diced
- 2 carrots, diced
- 1 cup frozen peas
- 2 cups mashed potatoes

Equipment:

1. Knife
2. Cutting board
3. Potato masher
4. Baking dish
5. Skillet

Methods:

Step 1: Preheat the oven to 375°F.

Step 2: Cook 1 cup of lentils in 2 cups of water for about 15-20 minutes, until tender.

Step 3: In a separate pan, sauté chopped onions, garlic, carrots, and celery in olive oil until soft.

Step 4: Add in diced bell peppers, zucchini, and mushrooms and cook for another 5 minutes.

Step 5: Mix in the cooked lentils, tomato paste, vegetable broth, and season with salt, pepper, and herbs.

Step 6: Transfer the mixture to a baking dish and top with mashed sweet potatoes.

Step 7: Bake for 25-30 minutes, or until the sweet potatoes are golden brown.

Step 8: Serve and enjoy!

Helpful Tips:

1. Start by prepping all your ingredients before you begin cooking to make the process smoother.

2. Use dried lentils instead of canned for better texture and flavor.

3. Add a variety of vegetables like carrots, celery, and peas for a colorful and nutritious dish.

4. Season each component separately to ensure a well-balanced flavor profile.

5. Consider adding fresh herbs like thyme or rosemary for an extra burst of flavor.

6. Top the shepherd's pie with a mixture of mashed potatoes and cauliflower for a lighter twist.

7. Bake the pie until the top is golden brown and bubbly to ensure a deliciously crispy finish.

Baked ratatouille with Parmesan breadcrumbs

Ingredients:

- 2 medium zucchinis
- 1 small eggplant
- 2 bell peppers
- 1 onion
- 2 cloves of garlic
- 2 tomatoes
- 1/4 cup breadcrumbs
- 1/4 cup grated Parmesan
- Salt, pepper, olive oil

Equipment:

1. Knife
2. Cutting board
3. Baking dish
4. Mixing bowl
5. Grater
6. Oven

Methods:

Step 1: Preheat your oven to 400°F.

Step 2: Prepare the vegetables by slicing zucchini, yellow squash, eggplant, and tomatoes into thin rounds.

Step 3: Arrange the sliced vegetables in a baking dish, alternating the different types.

Step 4: In a separate bowl, combine grated Parmesan cheese, breadcrumbs, and olive oil to make the topping.

Step 5: Sprinkle the Parmesan breadcrumbs mixture over the layered vegetables.

Step 6: Cover the baking dish with foil and bake for 30 minutes.

Step 7: Remove the foil and continue baking for an additional 15-20 minutes, or until the vegetables are tender.

Step 8: Serve hot and enjoy your delicious baked ratatouille!

Helpful Tips:

1. Slice your vegetables uniformly for even cooking.

2. Preheat your oven to ensure even baking.

3. Layer the vegetables in a baking dish in a single layer for a beautiful presentation.

4. Mix Parmesan cheese with breadcrumbs for a crunchy topping.

5. Drizzle olive oil over the vegetables before baking for added flavor and moisture.

6. Season generously with salt, pepper, and herbs for a flavorful dish.

7. Cover the baking dish with foil for the first part of baking to steam the vegetables.

8. Remove the foil towards the end to allow the breadcrumbs to crisp up.

9. Serve hot and enjoy a delicious, healthy meal.

Quinoa and vegetable stuffed portobello mushrooms

Ingredients:

- 4 large portobello mushrooms
- 1 cup quinoa
- 2 cups mixed vegetables
- 1/4 cup grated Parmesan cheese
- Salt and pepper to taste

Equipment:

1. Knife
2. Cutting board
3. Mixing bowl
4. Baking sheet
5. Saute pan

Methods:

Step 1: Preheat the oven to 375°F.

Step 2: Wash and de-stem the portobello mushrooms.

Step 3: In a large bowl, mix cooked quinoa with diced vegetables (such as bell peppers, onions, and zucchini).

Step 4: Drizzle the mushroom caps with olive oil, then spoon the quinoa and vegetable mixture into each cap.

Step 5: Place the stuffed mushrooms on a baking sheet and bake for 20-25 minutes, or until the mushrooms are tender.

Step 6: Remove from the oven and garnish with fresh herbs, such as parsley or basil.

Step 7: Serve hot and enjoy your delicious quinoa and vegetable stuffed portobello mushrooms!

Helpful Tips:

1. Preheat your oven to 375°F.
2. Wash and de-stem your portobello mushrooms.
3. Mix cooked quinoa with diced vegetables of your choice.

4. Season the quinoa and vegetable mixture with salt, pepper, and your favorite herbs or spices.

5. Fill each portobello mushroom with the quinoa and vegetable mixture.

6. Top each mushroom with a sprinkle of cheese if desired.

7. Place the stuffed mushrooms on a baking sheet lined with parchment paper.

8. Bake for 20-25 minutes, or until the mushrooms are tender.

9. Serve hot and enjoy your delicious and healthy meal!

Sweet potato and black bean chili

Ingredients:

- 2 sweet potatoes (cubed)
- 1 can of black beans
- 1 can of diced tomatoes
- 1 onion (diced)
- 2 cloves of garlic (minced)
- 1 tsp of cumin
- 1 tsp of chili powder
- 1/2 tsp of paprika
- Salt and pepper to taste

Equipment:

1. Large pot
2. Wooden spoon
3. Chef's knife
4. Cutting board
5. Can opener

Methods:

Step 1: Heat oil in a large pot over medium heat.

Step 2: Add chopped onions, bell peppers, and garlic. Cook until softened.

Step 3: Stir in chili powder, cumin, and paprika.

Step 4: Add chopped sweet potatoes and vegetable broth. Bring to a boil.

Step 5: Reduce heat and let simmer for 15-20 minutes, until sweet potatoes are tender.

Step 6: Stir in drained black beans, diced tomatoes, and corn.

Step 7: Let simmer for an additional 10 minutes.

Step 8: Season with salt and pepper to taste.

Step 9: Serve hot, garnished with chopped cilantro and a dollop of sour cream, if desired. Enjoy!

Helpful Tips:

1. Start by sautéing onions, garlic, and bell peppers in a large pot until they are soft.

2. Add diced sweet potatoes and cook until they begin to soften.

3. Stir in canned black beans, diced tomatoes, vegetable broth, and spices like chili powder, cumin, and paprika.

4. Allow the chili to simmer for at least 30 minutes to let the flavors meld together.

5. Adjust seasoning to taste with salt, pepper, and a squeeze of lime juice.

6. Serve hot with toppings like avocado, cilantro, and a dollop of Greek yogurt.

7. Enjoy with some cornbread or over rice for a complete meal.

Grilled chicken with pineapple salsa

Ingredients:
- 4 boneless chicken breasts
- 1/2 cup diced pineapple
- 1/4 cup diced red onion
- 1/4 cup chopped cilantro
- 1 tbsp lime juice
- Salt and pepper to taste

Equipment:
1. Grill
2. Cutting board
3. Knife
4. Mixing bowl
5. Tongs

Methods:
Step 1: Start by marinating the chicken breasts in a mixture of olive oil, lime juice, garlic, and your favorite seasonings.

Step 2: Preheat your grill to medium-high heat and oil the grates to prevent sticking.

Step 3: Grill the marinated chicken breasts for about 5-7 minutes per side, or until they reach an internal temperature of 165°F.

Step 4: While the chicken is cooking, prepare the pineapple salsa by combining diced pineapple, red onion, jalapeno, cilantro, lime juice, and salt in a bowl.

Step 5: Serve the grilled chicken topped with the pineapple salsa and enjoy!

Helpful Tips:
1. Marinate the chicken in a simple mixture of olive oil, garlic, lime juice, and herbs for at least 30 minutes before grilling.

2. Grill the chicken over medium heat for about 6-8 minutes per side, or until it reaches an internal temperature of 165°F.

3. While the chicken is cooking, prepare the pineapple salsa by combining diced pineapple, red onion, jalapeno, cilantro, lime juice, and salt.

4. Let the chicken rest for a few minutes before slicing and serving with a generous spoonful of the pineapple salsa on top.

5. Enjoy your flavorful and healthy grilled chicken with pineapple salsa!

Quinoa and vegetable stir fry

Ingredients:

- 1 cup quinoa
- 2 cups mixed vegetables
- 1/4 cup soy sauce
- 2 tbsp olive oil
- 1 tsp minced garlic
- 1 tsp ginger
- Salt and pepper to taste

Equipment:

1. Skillet
2. Saucepan
3. Chef's knife
4. Cutting board
5. Wooden spoon

Methods:

Step 1: Rinse 1 cup of quinoa under cold water and cook according to package instructions.

Step 2: Heat 1 tablespoon of olive oil in a large skillet over medium heat.

Step 3: Add 1 diced onion, 2 minced garlic cloves, and 1 diced bell pepper to the skillet. Cook for 5 minutes.

Step 4: Stir in 1 cup of chopped broccoli florets, 1 cup of sliced mushrooms, and 1 cup of sliced carrots. Cook for another 5 minutes.

Step 5: Add cooked quinoa to the skillet and stir to combine.

Step 6: Season with salt, pepper, and any desired herbs or spices.

Step 7: Serve hot and enjoy!

Helpful Tips:

1. Rinse the quinoa thoroughly before cooking to remove any bitter taste.

2. Use a ratio of 1 part quinoa to 2 parts water for cooking.

3. Cook the quinoa in a pot on the stove or in a rice cooker for about 15 minutes, or until all the water is absorbed.

4. Season the quinoa with salt, pepper, and any other desired spices before adding to the stir fry.

5. Use a variety of colorful vegetables such as bell peppers, broccoli, and carrots for added nutrition and flavor.

6. Stir fry the vegetables in a hot pan with a little oil until they are tender-crisp.

7. Mix in the cooked quinoa and stir well to combine all the ingredients.

8. Serve hot and enjoy your delicious and healthy quinoa and vegetable stir fry!

Tofu and vegetable spring rolls

Ingredients:

- 8 oz firm tofu
- 1 red bell pepper
- 1 carrot
- 4 oz bean sprouts
- 8 spring roll wrappers

Equipment:

1. Chef's knife
2. Cutting board
3. Frying pan
4. Rolling pin
5. Mixing bowls

Methods:

Step 1: Soak rice paper wrappers in warm water for 15-20 seconds to soften

Step 2: Lay out softened wrapper on a clean surface.

Step 3: Place thinly sliced tofu and a variety of sliced vegetables in the center of the wrapper.

Step 4: Fold the bottom of the wrapper over the filling, then fold in the sides.

Step 5: Continue rolling the wrapper until the filling is completely enclosed.

Step 6: Repeat with remaining wrappers and filling.

Step 7: Serve with a side of dipping sauce such as peanut or sweet chili sauce.

Step 8: Enjoy your homemade tofu and vegetable spring rolls!

Helpful Tips:

1. Press the tofu before using it to remove excess water and improve its texture.

2. Cut the tofu into small cubes or strips for easier rolling.

3. Marinate the tofu in a flavorful sauce or seasoning before adding it to the spring rolls.

4. Use a variety of fresh vegetables like carrot, cucumber, bell pepper, and lettuce for added crunch and flavor.

5. Soften the rice paper wrappers in warm water before assembling the spring rolls to make them easier to roll.

6. Serve the spring rolls with a dipping sauce like hoisin, peanut, or soy sauce for extra flavor.

7. Experiment with different herbs and spices to customize the flavor profile of your spring rolls.

Turkey and bean chili

Ingredients:
- 1 lb ground turkey
- 1 can of black beans
- 1 can of diced tomatoes
- 1 onion

Equipment:
1. Wooden spoon
2. Chef's knife
3. Saucepan
4. Skillet
5. Tongs

Methods:
Step 1: Heat olive oil in a large pot over medium heat.

Step 2: Add diced onion and minced garlic and cook until softened.

Step 3: Stir in ground turkey and cook until browned.

Step 4: Add chili powder, cumin, paprika, and salt.

Step 5: Pour in diced tomatoes, tomato sauce, and chicken broth.

Step 6: Add drained and rinsed kidney beans and black beans.

Step 7: Let simmer for 20-30 minutes, stirring occasionally.

Step 8: Taste and adjust seasoning as needed.

Step 9: Serve hot with toppings like shredded cheese, sour cream, and chopped cilantro. Enjoy your Turkey and bean chili!

Helpful Tips:
1. Start by browning the ground turkey in a large pot with diced onions and minced garlic for added flavor.

2. Add in your favorite beans (such as black beans or kidney beans) and diced tomatoes for a hearty base.

3. Season with chili powder, cumin, paprika, and salt to taste.

4. Feel free to add in additional ingredients like corn, bell peppers, or jalapenos for extra heat and texture.

5. Let the chili simmer on low heat for at least an hour to allow the flavors to meld together.

6. Serve hot with your choice of toppings such as shredded cheese, sour cream, or fresh cilantro. Enjoy!

Lentil and vegetable stuffed peppers

Ingredients:

- 4 large bell peppers
- 1 cup cooked lentils
- 1 cup diced vegetables
- 1/2 cup vegetable broth
- Salt and pepper to taste

Equipment:

1. Knife
2. Cutting board
3. Skillet
4. Wooden spoon
5. Baking dish

Methods:

Step 1: Preheat your oven to 375°F.

Step 2: Cut the tops off of the bell peppers and remove the seeds and membranes.

Step 3: In a large skillet, heat olive oil over medium heat.

Step 4: Add diced onion, garlic, and diced vegetables like zucchini and carrots. Cook until softened.

Step 5: Add cooked lentils, cooked rice, tomato sauce, and season with salt, pepper, and any other desired herbs and spices.

Step 6: Stuff the peppers with the lentil and vegetable mixture.

Step 7: Place the stuffed peppers in a baking dish and cover with foil.

Step 8: Bake for 25-30 minutes until peppers are tender.

Helpful Tips:

1. Begin by preheating your oven to 375°F.

2. Prepare your lentils according to package instructions and set aside.

3. Cut the tops off of your bell peppers and remove the seeds and membranes.

4. In a large skillet, sauté onions, garlic, and your choice of vegetables in olive oil until softened.

5. Mix in cooked lentils, cooked rice, and seasonings of your choice.

6. Stuff each bell pepper with the lentil and vegetable mixture.

7. Place stuffed peppers in a baking dish and cover with foil.

8. Bake for 25-30 minutes, or until the peppers are tender.

9. Serve and enjoy your delicious Lentil and vegetable stuffed peppers!

Baked salmon with garlic and herbs

Ingredients:

- 4 salmon fillets
- 4 cloves of garlic, minced
- 2 tbsp olive oil
- 1 tbsp fresh herbs (such as parsley or dill)
- Salt and pepper, to taste

Equipment:

1. Baking dish
2. Mixing bowl
3. Knife
4. Cutting board
5. Garlic press
6. Oven mitts

Methods:

Step 1: Preheat the oven to 375°F.

Step 2: Place the salmon fillet on a baking sheet lined with parchment paper.

Step 3: In a small bowl, mix together minced garlic, fresh herbs (such as dill parsley, and thyme), olive oil, lemon juice, salt, and pepper.

Step 4: Spread the herb mixture evenly over the salmon fillet.

Step 5: Bake the salmon in the preheated oven for 15-20 minutes, or until the salmon flakes easily with a fork.

Step 6: Remove the salmon from the oven and let it rest for a few minutes before serving.

Step 7: Enjoy your delicious baked salmon with garlic and herbs!

Helpful Tips:

1. Preheat the oven to 400°F.

2. Place the salmon fillet on a baking sheet lined with parchment paper.

3. In a small bowl, mix together minced garlic, chopped fresh herbs (such as dill, parsley, or thyme), olive oil, salt, and pepper.

4. Spread the herb mixture evenly over the salmon.

5. Bake the salmon for 12-15 minutes, or until it flakes easily with a fork.

6. Serve the baked salmon hot with a squeeze of lemon juice.

7. You can also add some thinly sliced lemon or additional fresh herbs for garnish.

8. Enjoy this delicious and nutritious dish!

Creamy cauliflower soup with chives

Ingredients:

- 1 head cauliflower
- 4 cups vegetable broth
- 1 onion, chopped
- 2 cloves garlic
- 1/2 cup heavy cream
- Salt and pepper
- Chopped chives

Equipment:

1. Large pot
2. Blender
3. Knife
4. Cutting board
5. Ladle

Methods:

Step 1: In a large pot, heat olive oil over medium heat.

Step 2: Add chopped onions and garlic, cook until softened.

Step 3: Add chopped cauliflower florets and vegetable broth.

Step 4: Bring to a boil, then reduce heat and simmer until cauliflower is tender.

Step 5: Blend with an immersion blender until smooth.

Step 6: Stir in heavy cream and season with salt and pepper.

Step 7: Simmer for a few more minutes.

Step 8: Serve hot, garnished with chopped chives.

Step 9: Enjoy your creamy cauliflower soup with chives!

Helpful Tips:

1. Start by sautéing diced onions and garlic in a large pot until fragrant.

2. Add chopped cauliflower florets and vegetable broth to the pot, then bring to a boil.

3. Reduce heat and simmer until cauliflower is softened.

4. Use an immersion blender to puree the soup until smooth and creamy.

5. Stir in heavy cream or coconut milk for a rich texture.

6. Season with salt, pepper, and any other desired spices.

7. Garnish each bowl with fresh chives for added flavor and a pop of color.

8. Serve hot with crusty bread or a side salad for a complete meal.

Teriyaki chicken and vegetable skewers

Ingredients:

- 1 lb chicken breast
- 1 cup Teriyaki sauce
- 2 bell peppers
- 1 zucchini

Equipment:

1. Skewers
2. Grill or stovetop pan
3. Mixing bowl
4. Tongs
5. Cutting board
6. Knife

Methods:

Step 1: Soak wooden skewers in water for at least 30 minutes to prevent burning.

Step 2: Cut chicken breasts into bite-sized chunks and mix with teriyaki sauce in a bowl.

Step 3: Cut bell peppers, zucchini, and onions into similar-sized pieces.

Step 4: Thread chicken and vegetables onto the soaked skewers, alternating between each ingredient.

Step 5: Preheat grill to medium-high heat.

Step 6: Grill skewers for about 10-12 minutes, turning occasionally and basting with extra teriyaki sauce.

Step 7: Serve hot with rice and enjoy your delicious teriyaki chicken and vegetable skewers.

Helpful Tips:

1. Marinate the chicken in teriyaki sauce for at least 30 minutes to allow the flavors to infuse.

2. Soak wooden skewers in water for at least 30 minutes to prevent them from burning on the grill.

3. Cut the chicken and vegetables into similar sized pieces for even cooking.

4. Alternate threading the chicken and vegetables onto the skewers for a colorful presentation.

5. Cook the skewers on a medium-high heat grill, turning them occasionally to ensure they cook evenly.

6. Baste the skewers with extra teriyaki sauce while cooking for added flavor.

7. Serve the skewers hot off the grill with a side of steamed rice for a complete meal.

Black bean and corn salad with lime vinaigrette

Ingredients:

- 1 can black beans
- 1 cup corn
- 1/4 cup red onion
- 1/4 cup cilantro
- 2 tbsp olive oil
- Juice of 1 lime
- Salt and pepper

Equipment:

1. Mixing bowl
2. Whisk
3. Cutting board
4. Knife
5. Serving bowl

Methods:

Step 1: In a large mixing bowl, combine 1 can of black beans (rinsed and drained) and 1 cup of frozen corn (thawed).

Step 2: Add 1 diced red bell pepper, 1 diced avocado, and 1/4 cup of chopped cilantro to the bowl.

Step 3: In a separate small bowl, whisk together 1/4 cup of olive oil, 2 tablespoons of lime juice, 1 tablespoon of honey, and salt and pepper to taste to make the vinaigrette.

Step 4: Pour the vinaigrette over the bean and corn mixture and gently toss to combine.

Step 5: Refrigerate for at least 30 minutes before serving. Enjoy your refreshing black bean and corn salad with lime vinaigrette!

Helpful Tips:

1. Rinse and drain the canned black beans and corn to remove excess sodium and preservatives.

2. Dice your favorite fresh vegetables, such as bell peppers, red onions, and cherry tomatoes, for added color and flavor.

3. Mix together olive oil, lime juice, minced garlic, salt, pepper, and a touch of honey for a zesty vinaigrette.

4. Toss the black beans, corn, and vegetables in the vinaigrette until evenly coated.

5. Let the salad marinate in the refrigerator for at least 30 minutes to allow the flavors to meld together.

6. Serve the salad chilled as a side dish or on top of a bed of greens for a complete meal. Enjoy!

Turkey and black bean burrito bowls

Ingredients:
- 1 lb ground turkey
- 1 can black beans
- 1 cup cooked rice
- 1 avocado
- 1/2 cup salsa
- 1/4 cup shredded cheese
- 1 tsp cumin
- 1 tsp paprika

Equipment:
1. Skillet
2. Wooden spatula
3. Mixing bowl
4. Cutting board
5. Chef's knife

Methods:
Step 1: Start by cooking the rice according to package instructions.

Step 2: While the rice is cooking, season ground turkey with your favorite taco seasoning and cook in a skillet until browned.

Step 3: Add black beans to the skillet with the turkey and heat through.

Step 4: Once the rice is done, divide it among bowls.

Step 5: Top the rice with the turkey and black bean mixture.

Step 6: Add your favorite toppings such as shredded cheese, diced tomatoes, sliced avocado, and cilantro.

Step 7: Serve and enjoy your delicious Turkey and black bean burrito bowls!

Helpful Tips:
1. Start by marinating the turkey with Mexican spices for added flavor.
2. Cook the beans with garlic, onion, and cumin for a tasty black bean base.

3. Use a variety of toppings such as avocado, salsa, and cheese for a customizable bowl.

4. Don't forget to add fresh cilantro and lime juice for a burst of freshness.

5. To save time, prep all your ingredients ahead of time to streamline the cooking process.

6. Use a rice cooker to easily prepare fluffy rice for the bowls.

7. Serve with a side of tortilla chips for added crunch.

8. Don't be afraid to experiment with different ingredients to create your own unique twist on the classic burrito bowl.

Eggplant and zucchini lasagna

Ingredients:
- 1 large eggplant
- 2 medium zucchinis
- 1 cup marinara sauce
- 1 cup grated mozzarella cheese
- 1/2 cup grated Parmesan cheese
- 1/4 cup chopped fresh basil leaves

Equipment:
1. Chef's knife
2. Cutting board
3. Baking dish
4. Skillet
5. Mixing bowl

Methods:
Step 1: Preheat the oven to 375°F.

Step 2: Slice one large eggplant and two zucchinis into thin rounds.

Step 3: In a large skillet, heat olive oil over medium heat and sauté the eggplant and zucchini slices until tender.

Step 4: In a separate bowl, mix together ricotta cheese, shredded mozzarella, grated Parmesan, one egg, and chopped fresh basil.

Step 5: In a baking dish, layer the cooked vegetables with marinara sauce and the cheese mixture.

Step 6: Repeat the layers until all ingredients are used, finishing with a layer of marinara and cheese.

Step 7: Cover with foil and bake for 30 minutes, then remove foil and bake for another 15 minutes until bubbly and golden brown. Enjoy your delicious eggplant and zucchini lasagna!

Helpful Tips:
1. Slice the eggplant and zucchini thinly to ensure even cooking.

2. Salt the sliced vegetables and let them sit for 20-30 minutes to draw out excess moisture and bitterness.

3. Precook the vegetables by grilling or roasting them before layering in the lasagna.

4. Use a flavorful tomato sauce to enhance the taste of the vegetables.

5. Layer the vegetables with a mixture of ricotta cheese, parmesan, and herbs for added creaminess.

6. Top the lasagna with mozzarella cheese for a gooey, melted finish.

7. Bake the lasagna at a lower temperature (around 350°F) for a longer time to ensure the vegetables are cooked through.

Seared tuna with sesame ginger glaze

Ingredients:

- 4 tuna steaks
- 1/4 cup soy sauce
- 2 tbsp honey
- 1 tbsp ginger, grated
- 2 tbsp sesame oil
- 2 cloves garlic, minced
- 1 tbsp sesame seeds

Equipment:

1. Skillet
2. Spatula
3. Tongs
4. Whisk
5. Basting brush
6. Kitchen knife

Methods:

Step 1: Marinate tuna steaks in a mixture of soy sauce, sesame oil, ginger and garlic for 30 minutes.

Step 2: Heat a skillet over high heat and add sesame oil.

Step 3: Sear tuna steaks for 1-2 minutes on each side until they are browned on the outside but still pink in the middle.

Step 4: Remove tuna from skillet and set aside.

Step 5: In the same skillet, add soy sauce, honey, rice vinegar, ginger, and sesame seeds to make the glaze.

Step 6: Simmer the glaze until it thickens, then drizzle over the seared tuna steaks.

Step 7: Serve hot and enjoy your delicious seared tuna with sesame ginger glaze.

Helpful Tips:

1. Start with high-quality sushi-grade tuna to ensure the best flavor and texture.

2. Pat the tuna dry with paper towels before cooking to ensure a nice sear.

3. Season the tuna with salt and pepper just before cooking for maximum flavor.

4. Heat a non-stick pan over high heat and add a small amount of oil before adding the tuna.

5. Cook the tuna for about 1-2 minutes per side for a rare to medium-rare doneness.

6. Brush the tuna with a sesame ginger glaze while cooking for extra flavor.

7. Let the tuna rest for a few minutes before slicing and serving to allow the juices to redistribute.

Chickpea and vegetable stir fry

Ingredients:
- 1 can of chickpeas
- 1 red bell pepper
- 1 zucchini
- 1 carrot
- 1 onion
- 2 cloves of garlic
- 1 tbsp olive oil
- 2 tbsp soy sauce
- Salt and pepper to taste

Equipment:
1. Saucepan
2. Wooden spoon
3. Chef's knife
4. Cutting board
5. Stirring spoon

Methods:
Step 1: Heat 1 tablespoon of oil in a pan over medium heat.

Step 2: Add 1 chopped onion and sauté for 2-3 minutes until translucent.

Step 3: Add 2 minced garlic cloves and cook for another minute.

Step 4: Stir in 1 diced bell pepper, 1 diced zucchini, and 1 can of drained chickpeas.

Step 5: Season with salt, pepper, and desired spices (such as cumin or paprika).

Step 6: Cook for 5-7 minutes until vegetables are tender.

Step 7: Serve hot over rice or quinoa, garnished with fresh herbs if desired. Enjoy your delicious chickpea and vegetable stir fry!

Helpful Tips:
1. Start by sautéing diced onions and garlic in a large skillet until fragrant.

2. Add your favorite vegetables such as bell peppers, zucchini, and mushrooms to the skillet.

3. Stir in cooked chickpeas and your choice of seasonings like cumin, paprika, and turmeric for added flavor.

4. For a sauce, mix together soy sauce, sesame oil, and a splash of rice vinegar to drizzle over the stir-fry.

5. Cook until vegetables are tender but still slightly crisp, approximately 5-7 minutes.

6. Serve over cooked rice or quinoa for a complete and nutritious meal. Enjoy your delicious chickpea and vegetable stir-fry!

Quinoa and black bean stuffed bell peppers

Ingredients:

- 1 cup quinoa
- 2 cups black beans
- 4 bell peppers
- 1 cup corn
- 1/2 cup diced tomatoes
- 1/4 cup diced onions
- 2 tsp taco seasoning

Equipment:

1. Knife
2. Cutting board
3. Skillet
4. Mixing bowl
5. Wooden spoon

Methods:

Step 1: Preheat the oven to 375°F.

Step 2: Cook quinoa according to package instructions.

Step 3: In a large skillet, heat olive oil over medium heat.

Step 4: Add diced onion, minced garlic, and diced bell peppers to the skillet.

Step 5: Cook until vegetables are softened, about 5 minutes.

Step 6: Stir in black beans, cooked quinoa, diced tomatoes, and seasonings.

Step 7: Cut bell peppers in half lengthwise and remove seeds.

Step 8: Place the bell pepper halves in a baking dish.

Step 9: Spoon the quinoa mixture into each pepper half.

Step 10: Cover with foil and bake for 25 minutes. Serve hot and enjoy!

Helpful Tips:

1. Start by cooking the quinoa according to package instructions for best results.

2. Rinse the black beans thoroughly to remove excess sodium and improve flavor.

3. Use a variety of colorful bell peppers for a visually appealing dish.

4. Consider adding spices like cumin, chili powder, and garlic for extra flavor.

5. Add in diced vegetables like onions, corn, and tomatoes for texture and nutrition.

6. Top with a sprinkle of cheese before baking for a gooey, melty finish.

7. For a vegan option, skip the cheese or use a plant-based alternative.

8. Serve with a dollop of Greek yogurt or avocado for added creaminess.

9. Don't forget to season with salt and pepper to taste before serving.

Ratatouille with lentils

Ingredients:

- 1 cup lentils
- 1 eggplant
- 2 zucchinis
- 1 red bell pepper
- 1 onion
- 2 garlic cloves
- 1 can diced tomatoes
- 1 tsp dried thyme
- 1 tsp dried oregano
- 1/2 tsp salt
- 1/4 tsp black pepper

Equipment:

1. Skillet
2. Saucepan
3. Chef's knife
4. Cutting board
5. Wooden spoon
6. Tongs

Methods:

Step 1: Rinse 1 cup of lentils under cold water and cook them according to package instructions.

Step 2: Heat 2 tablespoons of olive oil in a large pan over medium heat.

Step 3: Add 1 diced onion and sauté until softened, about 5 minutes.

Step 4: Stir in 2 cloves of minced garlic and cook for another minute.

Step 5: Add 1 diced eggplant, 1 diced zucchini, 1 diced bell pepper, and 1 can of diced tomatoes.

Step 6: Season with salt, pepper, and dried herbs like thyme and oregano.

Step 7: Cover and let simmer for 20 minutes.

Step 8: Serve the ratatouille over the cooked lentils. Enjoy!

Helpful Tips:

1. Start by sautéing onions and garlic in olive oil until soft.

2. Add diced vegetables like zucchini, bell peppers, and eggplant.

3. Stir in canned tomatoes, lentils, and vegetable broth.

4. Season with dried herbs like thyme, oregano, and basil.

5. Simmer the mixture for at least 20-30 minutes to allow flavors to meld.

6. Serve over cooked quinoa or rice for a complete meal.

7. Garnish with fresh parsley or basil before serving for a pop of color.

8. Consider adding some red pepper flakes for a kick of heat.

Note: Adjust seasoning and consistency as needed throughout the cooking process. Enjoy your healthy and delicious Ratatouille with lentils!

Grilled vegetable quesadillas with whole wheat tortillas

Ingredients:

- 1 zucchini, sliced
- 1 red bell pepper, sliced
- 1 yellow onion, sliced
- 1 cup grated cheese
- 4 whole wheat tortillas

Equipment:

1. Skillet
2. Spatula
3. Knife
4. Cutting board
5. Grater

Methods:

Step 1: Preheat your grill to medium-high heat.

Step 2: Brush sliced vegetables (such as bell peppers, zucchini, and red onion) with olive oil and season with salt and pepper.

Step 3: Grill the vegetables until they are tender and slightly charred, about 3-4 minutes per side.

Step 4: Remove the vegetables from the grill and chop them into bite-sized pieces.

Step 5: Place a whole wheat tortilla on a flat surface and sprinkle with shredded cheese.

Step 6: Add the grilled vegetables on top of the cheese.

Step 7: Top with another whole wheat tortilla and press down gently.

Step 8: Grill the quesadilla until the cheese is melted and the tortillas are crispy, about 2-3 minutes per side.

Step 9: Cut the quesadilla into wedges and serve with salsa and sour cream on the side. Enjoy!

Helpful Tips:

1. Preheat your grill to medium-high heat and lightly oil the grates.

2. Slice your favorite vegetables, such as bell peppers, zucchini, and onions, into thin strips for even cooking.

3. Season the vegetables with olive oil, salt, pepper, and any other desired seasonings.

4. Grill the vegetables until they are slightly charred and tender, about 5-7 minutes per side.

5. Lay out a whole wheat tortilla and sprinkle with shredded cheese, the grilled vegetables, and another layer of cheese.

6. Top with another tortilla and grill for 2-3 minutes per side, until the cheese is melted and the tortilla is crispy.

7. Serve hot with salsa, guacamole, or Greek yogurt for dipping. Enjoy!

Lemon herb tilapia with green beans

Ingredients:

- 4 tilapia fillets
- 1 lemon
- 2 tbsp olive oil
- 2 tsp dried herbs
- 1 lb green beans
- Salt and pepper to taste

Equipment:

1. Skillet
2. Tongs
3. Knife
4. Cutting board
5. Baking dish

Methods:

Step 1: Preheat your oven to 400°F

Step 2: Season the tilapia fillets with salt, pepper, lemon juice, and chopped herbs (such as parsley or dill)

Step 3: Place the seasoned tilapia fillets on a baking sheet and bake for 12-15 minutes, or until the fish is cooked through and flakes easily with a fork

Step 4: In a separate pan, sauté the green beans with olive oil, garlic, salt, and pepper until they are tender-crisp

Step 5: Serve the cooked tilapia fillets with the sautéed green beans on the side

Step 6: Enjoy your delicious and healthy lemon herb tilapia with green beans!

Helpful Tips:

1. Preheat the oven to 400°F.

2. Season the tilapia fillets with lemon juice, minced garlic, chopped parsley, salt, and pepper.

3. Place the seasoned fillets on a baking sheet and bake for 10-12 minutes or until the fish is flaky.

4. In a separate pan, sauté green beans with olive oil, minced garlic, salt, and pepper until tender.

5. Serve the baked tilapia on a plate with the sautéed green beans on the side.

6. Garnish with lemon slices and fresh herbs for extra flavor.

7. Enjoy your delicious and healthy meal!

Lentil and vegetable stuffed cabbage rolls

Ingredients:
- 1 head of cabbage
- 1 cup cooked lentils
- 1 carrot, grated
- 1 onion, diced
- 2 cloves of garlic, minced
- 1 can of diced tomatoes
- 1 teaspoon of cumin
- Salt and pepper to taste

Equipment:
1. Mixing bowl
2. Cutting board
3. Knife
4. Saucepan
5. Cooking pot

Methods:
Step 1: Boil a large pot of water and blanch cabbage leaves until soft.

Step 2: Cook lentils according to package instructions and set aside.

Step 3: In a separate pan, sauté onions, carrots, and garlic until softened.

Step 4: Combine cooked lentils, vegetables, and seasonings in a bowl.

Step 5: Place a spoonful of filling onto each cabbage leaf and roll up tightly

Step 6: Place cabbage rolls in a baking dish and cover with tomato sauce.

Step 7: Bake in the oven at 375°F for 25-30 minutes.

Step 8: Serve hot and enjoy your Lentil and vegetable stuffed cabbage rolls

Helpful Tips:
1. Start by boiling a large head of cabbage until the leaves are tender and easy to peel off.

2. Prepare a filling with cooked lentils, minced vegetables, such as carrots onions, and celery, and season with herbs and spices like garlic, thyme, and paprika.

3. Place a spoonful of filling onto each cabbage leaf and roll tightly, tucking in the sides as you go.

4. Arrange the cabbage rolls in a baking dish and top with a tomato-based sauce before baking in the oven until heated through.

5. Serve hot with a side of rice or crusty bread for a satisfying and nutritious meal.

Spicy chickpea and vegetable curry

Ingredients:

- 1 can of chickpeas
- 1 red bell pepper
- 1 zucchini
- 1 can of diced tomatoes
- 1 onion
- 2 cloves of garlic
- 1 tsp of cumin
- 1 tsp of turmeric
- 1/2 tsp of red pepper flakes
- 1 cup of vegetable broth

Equipment:

1. Pot
2. Pan
3. Spatula
4. Knife
5. Cutting board

Methods:

Step 1: Heat oil in a large pot over medium heat

Step 2: Add diced onion and cook until translucent

Step 3: Stir in minced garlic and grated ginger

Step 4: Add curry powder, cumin, coriander, and turmeric

Step 5: Cook for 1 minute until fragrant

Step 6: Stir in chopped tomatoes and vegetable broth

Step 7: Bring to a simmer and add drained chickpeas

Step 8: Add chopped vegetables such as bell peppers, carrots, and potatoes

Step 9: Simmer for 15-20 minutes until vegetables are tender

Step 10: Season with salt, pepper, and red pepper flakes

Step 11: Serve over rice or with naan bread. Enjoy!

Helpful Tips:

1. Start by heating oil in a large skillet or pot over medium heat.

2. Add in diced onions, bell peppers, carrots, and garlic. Cook until vegetables are soft.

3. Stir in diced tomatoes, chickpeas, and vegetable broth.

4. Mix in curry powder, cumin, turmeric, and paprika. Adjust seasonings to taste.

5. Let the curry simmer for about 15-20 minutes to allow the flavors to meld together.

6. Serve over rice or with naan bread for a complete meal.

7. Garnish with fresh cilantro and a squeeze of lime juice for an added burst of flavor.

8. Enjoy your spicy chickpea and vegetable curry!

Turkey and vegetable meatloaf

Ingredients:

- 1 lb ground turkey
- 1 cup chopped mixed vegetables
- 1/2 cup breadcrumbs
- 1 egg

Equipment:

1. Mixing bowl
2. Baking dish
3. Knife
4. Cutting board
5. Spatula

Methods:

Step 1: Preheat the oven to 375°F.

Step 2: In a large mixing bowl, combine ground turkey, diced vegetables (carrots, celery, onions), bread crumbs, Worcestershire sauce, ketchup, and seasonings.

Step 3: Mix all ingredients thoroughly until well combined.

Step 4: Transfer the mixture to a loaf pan and shape into a loaf.

Step 5: Bake in the preheated oven for 45-50 minutes or until the internal temperature reaches 165°F.

Step 6: Let the meatloaf rest for 10 minutes before slicing and serving.

Step 7: Enjoy your delicious and nutritious turkey and vegetable meatloaf!

Helpful Tips:

1. Use lean ground turkey to keep the meatloaf moist without adding extra fat.

2. Incorporate plenty of finely chopped vegetables like onions, bell peppers, and carrots for added flavor and nutrition.

3. Add breadcrumbs or oats to help bind the meatloaf mixture together.

4. Don't overmix the ingredients to keep the meatloaf tender.

5. Season generously with herbs and spices like garlic powder, thyme, and paprika.

6. Consider adding a topping like ketchup or barbecue sauce for extra flavor.

7. Bake at a moderate temperature (about 350°F) until cooked through, typically around 45-60 minutes.

8. Let the meatloaf rest for a few minutes before slicing and serving.

Cauliflower and white bean soup

Ingredients:

- 1 head of cauliflower
- 1 can of white beans
- 1 onion
- 2 cloves of garlic
- 4 cups of vegetable broth
- Salt and pepper to taste

Equipment:

1. Pot
2. Ladle
3. Blender
4. Knife
5. Cutting board

Methods:

Step 1: In a large pot, heat olive oil over medium heat.

Step 2: Add chopped onions and garlic, sauté until soft.

Step 3: Add diced potatoes and cauliflower florets, cook for a few minutes.

Step 4: Pour in vegetable broth and bring to a boil.

Step 5: Reduce heat and let simmer until vegetables are tender.

Step 6: Add white beans and season with salt, pepper, and herbs.

Step 7: Use an immersion blender to partially blend soup, leaving some chunks for texture.

Step 8: Serve hot with a drizzle of olive oil and a sprinkle of fresh parsley Enjoy!

Helpful Tips:

1. Start by sautéing onion, garlic, and celery in olive oil until softened.

2. Add chopped cauliflower and cook until slightly browned.

3. Pour in vegetable broth and bring to a boil, then reduce heat and simmer until cauliflower is tender.

4. Add in drained white beans and season with salt, pepper, and any desired herbs or spices.

5. Use a blender to puree the soup until smooth and creamy.

6. Thin with additional broth or water if needed.

7. Serve hot with a drizzle of olive oil, a sprinkle of Parmesan cheese, and fresh herbs on top.

8. Enjoy with crusty bread or a side salad for a complete meal.

Lemon garlic salmon with asparagus

Ingredients:
- 4 salmon fillets
- 1 lemon
- 4 cloves of garlic
- 1 bunch of asparagus
- Salt and pepper to taste

Equipment:
1. Frying pan
2. Spatula
3. Tongs
4. Baking sheet
5. Aluminum foil
6. Knife

Methods:
Step 1: Preheat your oven to 400°F.

Step 2: In a small bowl, mix together minced garlic, lemon juice, olive oil, salt, and pepper.

Step 3: Place salmon fillets on a baking sheet lined with parchment paper and brush with the garlic lemon mixture.

Step 4: Arrange asparagus spears around the salmon fillets and drizzle with olive oil, salt, and pepper.

Step 5: Bake in the preheated oven for 12-15 minutes, or until the salmon is cooked through and the asparagus is tender.

Step 6: Serve the lemon garlic salmon with roasted asparagus and enjoy!

Helpful Tips:
1. Start by preheating your oven to 400°F (200°C).

2. Season your salmon fillets with salt, pepper, garlic powder, and dried oregano.

3. In a small bowl, mix together melted butter, minced garlic, lemon juice, and lemon zest.

4. Place the salmon fillets on a baking sheet lined with foil, and pour the lemon garlic sauce over the top.

5. Arrange the asparagus spears around the salmon, drizzle with olive oil, and season with salt and pepper.

6. Bake in the preheated oven for 12-15 minutes, or until the salmon is cooked through and the asparagus is tender.

7. Serve hot and enjoy!

Roasted sweet potato and black bean tacos

Ingredients:

- 2 large sweet potatoes
- 1 can black beans
- 1 tsp cumin
- 1 tsp paprika
- 1/2 tsp garlic powder
- 1/2 tsp chili powder
- 8 small corn tortillas
- 1 avocado
- 1 lime

Equipment:

1. Knife
2. Cutting board
3. Skillet
4. Mixing bowl
5. Spatula

Methods:

Step 1: Preheat the oven to 400°F and line a baking sheet with parchment paper.

Step 2: Peel and dice 2 large sweet potatoes.

Step 3: Toss the sweet potatoes with olive oil, salt, pepper, and cumin.

Step 4: Spread the sweet potatoes in an even layer on the baking sheet.

Step 5: Roast the sweet potatoes for 25-30 minutes, or until tender and slightly caramelized.

Step 6: Rinse and drain a can of black beans.

Step 7: Heat the black beans in a saucepan with a splash of water and cumin.

Step 8: Assemble the tacos with roasted sweet potatoes, black beans, avocado, and salsa. Enjoy!

Helpful Tips:

1. Preheat your oven to 400°F.

2. Peel and dice the sweet potatoes into small cubes.

3. Toss the sweet potatoes with olive oil, salt, pepper, and your favorite taco seasoning.

4. Spread the sweet potatoes on a baking sheet and roast in the oven for 20-25 minutes, or until tender.

5. Rinse and drain a can of black beans.

6. Heat the black beans in a skillet with some cumin, garlic powder, and a pinch of salt.

7. Warm up corn or flour tortillas in a pan or in the oven.

8. Assemble the tacos by filling the tortillas with the roasted sweet potatoes, black beans, and your favorite toppings like avocado, salsa, and cilantro. Enjoy!

Mediterranean chickpea and vegetable stew

Ingredients:

- 1 can of chickpeas, drained
- 1 red bell pepper, diced
- 1 zucchini, diced
- 1 onion, chopped
- 1 can of diced tomatoes
- 2 cloves of garlic, minced
- 1 tsp of cumin
- 1 tsp of paprika
- 1/2 tsp of turmeric
- 1/4 tsp of red pepper flakes
- 4 cups of vegetable broth
- Salt and pepper to taste

Equipment:

1. Dutch oven
2. Wooden spoon
3. Chef's knife
4. Cutting board
5. Ladle

Methods:

Step 1: Heat olive oil in a large pot over medium heat.

Step 2: Add chopped onion and sauté until translucent.

Step 3: Stir in minced garlic and cook for another minute.

Step 4: Add diced tomatoes, chickpeas, and vegetable broth to the pot.

Step 5: Season with salt, pepper, and your choice of Mediterranean spices.

Step 6: Cover and simmer for 20 minutes, stirring occasionally.

Step 7: Add chopped vegetables such as bell peppers, zucchini, and carrots to the stew.

Step 8: Cook for an additional 10-15 minutes until vegetables are tender.

Step 9: Serve hot with a sprinkle of fresh herbs on top. Enjoy your Mediterranean chickpea and vegetable stew!

Helpful Tips:

1. Start by sautéing onions and garlic in olive oil for extra flavor.

2. Use a mix of seasonal vegetables such as tomatoes, bell peppers, zucchini, and eggplant for a variety of textures and colors.

3. Add canned or cooked chickpeas for protein and fiber.

4. Season with Mediterranean herbs like oregano, thyme, and rosemary for an authentic taste.

5. Simmer the stew slowly to allow the flavors to meld together.

6. Serve with crusty bread or over couscous for a satisfying meal.

7. Garnish with fresh parsley or a drizzle of extra virgin olive oil before serving.

Cauliflower rice stir fry with tofu

Ingredients:

- 1 head cauliflower
- 1 block tofu
- 2 carrots
- 1 bell pepper
- 4 tbsp soy sauce
- 2 tbsp sesame oil
- 1 tbsp ginger
- 2 cloves garlic

Equipment:

1. Skillet
2. Spatula
3. Knife
4. Cutting board
5. Mixing bowl

Methods:

Step 1: Cut a head of cauliflower into florets and pulse in a food processor until it resembles rice.

Step 2: Press tofu to remove excess water, then cut into cubes.

Step 3: Heat oil in a large skillet and add tofu, cook until browned on all sides.

Step 4: Add chopped vegetables such as bell peppers, carrots, and peas to the skillet.

Step 5: Stir in the cauliflower rice and season with soy sauce, ginger, and garlic.

Step 6: Cook for 5-7 minutes, stirring frequently.

Step 7: Serve hot with chopped green onions and sesame seeds on top. Enjoy your delicious cauliflower rice stir fry with tofu!

Helpful Tips:

1. Start by pressing the tofu to remove excess moisture before cutting into cubes.

2. Use a non-stick pan or wok to stir fry the cauliflower rice and tofu to prevent sticking.

3. Add in your favorite vegetables like bell peppers, carrots, and snap peas for added flavor and nutrition.

4. Season with soy sauce, garlic, ginger, and a pinch of red pepper flakes for a delicious Asian-inspired taste.

5. Make sure to cook the cauliflower rice until it is tender but still slightly crunchy for the best texture.

6. Garnish with sesame seeds and green onions before serving for a fresh and aromatic finish.

Baked cod with tomato and caper relish

Ingredients:
- 4 cod fillets
- 2 cups cherry tomatoes
- 1/4 cup capers
- 2 cloves garlic
- 2 tbsp olive oil
- 1 lemon
- Salt and pepper to taste

Equipment:
1. Baking dish
2. Mixing bowl
3. Knife
4. Cutting board
5. Aluminum foil
6. Spoon

Methods:
Step 1: Preheat the oven to 400°F and grease a baking dish.

Step 2: Season the cod fillets with salt, pepper, and olive oil.

Step 3: Place the cod fillets in the prepared baking dish and bake for 15-20 minutes, or until the fish is cooked through.

Step 4: While the cod is baking, prepare the tomato and caper relish by mixing chopped tomatoes, capers, garlic, parsley, lemon juice, and olive oil in a bowl.

Step 5: Once the cod is done baking, spoon the relish over the top of the fish.

Step 6: Serve the baked cod with tomato and caper relish hot and enjoy!

Helpful Tips:
1. Start by preheating your oven to 400°F.
2. Rub the cod fillets with olive oil and season with salt and pepper.
3. Place the cod fillets on a baking sheet lined with parchment paper.

4. In a bowl, mix together diced tomatoes, capers, garlic, olive oil, and lemon juice to make the relish.

5. Spoon the relish over the cod fillets.

6. Bake in the preheated oven for 15-20 minutes, or until the cod is cooked through.

7. Serve hot with a side of roasted vegetables or a salad.

8. Garnish with fresh herbs like parsley or basil before serving. Enjoy!

Grilled chicken with roasted red pepper sauce

Ingredients:
- 4 chicken breasts
- 2 red bell peppers
- 1 onion
- 2 garlic cloves
- Olive oil
- Salt and pepper

Equipment:
1. Grill pan
2. Roasting pan
3. Tongs
4. Kitchen knife
5. Mixing bowl

Methods:
Step 1: Marinate chicken breasts in olive oil, garlic, and herbs for at least 30 minutes.

Step 2: Preheat grill to medium-high heat.

Step 3: Grill chicken for 6-8 minutes on each side or until cooked through

Step 4: In a blender, combine roasted red peppers, garlic, olive oil, salt, and pepper.

Step 5: Blend until smooth to create the red pepper sauce.

Step 6: Transfer chicken to serving plates and spoon red pepper sauce over the top.

Step 7: Serve hot and enjoy your delicious grilled chicken with roasted red pepper sauce.

Helpful Tips:
1. Start by marinating the chicken in olive oil, garlic, herbs, and lemon juice for at least an hour before grilling.

2. Preheat the grill to medium-high heat and make sure it's clean and well-oiled to prevent sticking.

3. Grill the chicken for about 6-8 minutes per side, or until cooked through with nice grill marks.

4. While the chicken is grilling, roast red peppers in the oven until charred, then peel and blend with olive oil, garlic, salt, and pepper to make the sauce.

5. Serve the grilled chicken with the roasted red pepper sauce drizzled on top for a flavorful and delicious meal.

Black bean and corn stuffed peppers

Ingredients:
- 4 large bell peppers
- 1 can black beans (15 oz)
- 1 cup corn kernels
- 1 cup cooked quinoa
- 1/2 cup salsa
- 1 tsp cumin
- 1/2 tsp chili powder
- Salt and pepper to taste

Equipment:
1. Chef's knife
2. Cutting board
3. Mixing bowl
4. Baking dish
5. Spoon
6. Skillet

Methods:
Step 1: Preheat the oven to 375°F.

Step 2: Cut the tops off of the bell peppers and remove the seeds and membranes.

Step 3: In a large bowl, mix together cooked black beans, corn, diced tomatoes, cooked quinoa, and spices.

Step 4: Stuff each pepper with the black bean mixture and place in a baking dish.

Step 5: Pour 1/4 cup of vegetable broth over the stuffed peppers.

Step 6: Cover the baking dish with foil and bake for 30 minutes.

Step 7: Remove the foil and bake for an additional 10 minutes.

Step 8: Serve the black bean and corn stuffed peppers hot with your favorite toppings.

Helpful Tips:

1. Cook the black beans and corn in a separate pan with some spices for added flavor.

2. Pre-cook the bell peppers by blanching them in boiling water for a few minutes to soften them before stuffing.

3. Consider adding diced tomatoes, onions, and garlic to the black bean and corn mixture for extra depth of flavor.

4. Top the stuffed peppers with shredded cheese before baking for a gooey, melty finish.

5. Drizzle some olive oil on top of the peppers before and after baking to keep them moist and prevent them from drying out.

6. Serve with a side of rice or quinoa for a complete meal.

Lemon herb shrimp and broccoli stir fry

Ingredients:
- 1 lb shrimp
- 1 head broccoli
- 2 tbsp olive oil
- 2 cloves garlic
- 1 lemon
- 1 tbsp dried herbs
- Salt and pepper to taste

Equipment:
1. Skillet
2. Tongs
3. Cutting board
4. Knife
5. Mixing bowl

Methods:
Step 1: Heat olive oil in a large skillet over medium heat.

Step 2: Add shrimp to the skillet and cook until they turn pink, about 2-3 minutes per side.

Step 3: Remove shrimp from skillet and set aside.

Step 4: Add broccoli florets to the same skillet and cook for about 3-4 minutes, until they begin to soften.

Step 5: Add minced garlic and lemon zest to the broccoli and cook for an additional minute.

Step 6: Return shrimp to the skillet and sprinkle with dried herbs (such as thyme, oregano, and parsley).

Step 7: Stir everything together and cook for another 1-2 minutes.

Step 8: Serve hot and enjoy!

Helpful Tips:
1. Start by marinating the shrimp in a mixture of lemon juice, garlic, and herbs for maximum flavor.

2. Make sure to cook the broccoli until it is tender but still crisp for the perfect texture.

3. Use a hot wok or skillet to quickly stir-fry the shrimp and broccoli to maintain their color and nutrients.

4. Add in a splash of chicken broth or white wine for extra moisture and flavor.

5. Season with salt, pepper, and red pepper flakes to taste before serving.

6. Garnish with fresh chopped parsley or cilantro for a pop of brightness.

7. Serve over steamed rice or quinoa for a complete meal.

Quinoa and black bean salad with lime dressing

Ingredients:

- 1 cup quinoa
- 1 can black beans, drained
- 1 red bell pepper, diced
- 1/4 cup chopped cilantro
- 2 tbsp olive oil
- 2 limes, juiced
- Salt and pepper to taste

Equipment:

1. Mixing bowl
2. Whisk
3. Cutting board
4. Knife
5. Salad spinner

Methods:

Step 1: Rinse 1 cup of quinoa in a fine-mesh sieve under cold water.

Step 2: In a medium saucepan, bring 2 cups of water and the rinsed quinoa to a boil.

Step 3: Reduce heat to low, cover, and simmer for 15 minutes or until quinoa is cooked.

Step 4: In a large bowl, combine the cooked quinoa, 1 can of black beans (rinsed and drained), 1 diced bell pepper, and 1/4 cup of finely chopped cilantro.

Step 5: In a small bowl, whisk together 1/4 cup of olive oil, 2 tablespoons of lime juice, 1 minced garlic clove, and salt and pepper to taste.

Step 6: Pour the dressing over the quinoa mixture and toss to combine.

Step 7: Serve the salad chilled or at room temperature. Enjoy!

Helpful Tips:

1. Rinse the quinoa thoroughly before cooking to remove any bitterness.

2. Cook the quinoa in vegetable or chicken broth instead of water for added flavor.

3. Make sure to drain and rinse the black beans before adding them to the salad.

4. To make the lime dressing, whisk together fresh lime juice, olive oil, honey, salt, and pepper.

5. Toss the cooked quinoa, black beans, diced tomatoes, chopped cilantro, and lime dressing together in a large bowl.

6. Let the salad sit in the fridge for at least 30 minutes before serving to allow the flavors to meld.

7. Serve chilled and garnish with extra cilantro and a lime wedge. Enjoy!

Grilled chicken with roasted vegetables

Ingredients:

- 4 chicken breasts
- 2 bell peppers
- 1 zucchini
- 1 red onion
- 1 tbsp olive oil
- 1 tsp salt
- 1 tsp pepper
- 1 tsp garlic powder

Equipment:

1. Tongs
2. Grill pan
3. Baking sheet
4. Chef's knife
5. Cutting board

Methods:

Step 1: Preheat the grill to medium-high heat.

Step 2: Season the chicken breasts with salt, pepper, and your favorite spices or marinade.

Step 3: Place the chicken on the grill and cook for 6-7 minutes per side, or until cooked through and no longer pink in the center.

Step 4: While the chicken is cooking, toss your favorite vegetables (such as bell peppers, zucchini, and onions) with olive oil, salt, and pepper.

Step 5: Spread the vegetables on a baking sheet and roast in the oven at 400°F for 20-25 minutes, or until tender.

Step 6: Serve the grilled chicken with the roasted vegetables and enjoy!

Helpful Tips:

1. Marinate the chicken with your favorite seasonings for at least 30 minutes to enhance the flavor.

2. Cut your vegetables into similar sizes to ensure even cooking.

3. Preheat your grill to medium-high heat before adding the chicken and vegetables.

4. Brush olive oil onto the vegetables before roasting to prevent sticking.

5. Cook the chicken until it reaches an internal temperature of 165°F to ensure it is fully cooked.

6. Rotate the vegetables occasionally to promote even roasting.

7. Serve the grilled chicken and roasted vegetables hot off the grill for the best flavor and texture.

Quinoa salad with lemon vinaigrette

Ingredients:
- 1 cup quinoa
- 2 cups water
- 1 lemon
- 1/4 cup olive oil
- Salt and pepper

Equipment:
1. Mixing bowl
2. Whisk
3. Salad tongs
4. Cutting board
5. Knife
6. Grater

Methods:
Step 1: Rinse 1 cup of quinoa in a fine mesh strainer to remove bitterness.

Step 2: In a medium saucepan, bring 2 cups of water to a boil.

Step 3: Add the rinsed quinoa to the boiling water, reduce heat to low, cover, and simmer for about 15 minutes.

Step 4: Remove from heat and let quinoa sit, covered, for 5 minutes.

Step 5: Fluff quinoa with a fork and transfer to a large mixing bowl.

Step 6: In a small bowl, whisk together 1/4 cup of olive oil, 2 tablespoons of lemon juice, 1 teaspoon of honey, and salt and pepper to taste to make the vinaigrette.

Step 7: Pour the vinaigrette over the quinoa and mix well to combine.

Step 8: Add chopped fresh vegetables of your choice, such as cucumbers, tomatoes, and bell peppers, to the quinoa and toss to combine.

Step 9: Refrigerate for at least 30 minutes before serving.

Helpful Tips:
1. Rinse the quinoa thoroughly before cooking to remove any bitter taste.

2. Cook the quinoa with a 1:2 ratio of quinoa to water for fluffy, perfectly cooked grains.

3. Let the quinoa cool before mixing it with the other salad ingredients to prevent it from getting mushy.

4. Prepare the lemon vinaigrette with fresh lemon juice, olive oil, honey, garlic, salt, and pepper for a bright, tangy flavor.

5. Toss the quinoa salad with the vinaigrette just before serving to keep it fresh and flavorful.

6. Add fresh herbs, chopped vegetables, and nuts for added texture and flavor.

Baked salmon with dill and lemon

Ingredients:
- 4 salmon fillets
- 2 tbsp chopped dill
- 1 lemon, thinly sliced
- Salt and pepper to taste
- Olive oil for drizzling

Equipment:
1. Baking dish
2. Whisk
3. Mixing bowl
4. Knife
5. Cutting board

Methods:
Step 1: Preheat the oven to 400°F and line a baking sheet with aluminum foil.

Step 2: Place a salmon fillet on the prepared baking sheet.

Step 3: Drizzle olive oil over the salmon and season with salt and pepper.

Step 4: Top the salmon with fresh dill and lemon slices.

Step 5: Cover the salmon with another sheet of aluminum foil and bake for 15-20 minutes, or until the salmon is cooked through.

Step 6: Remove the foil and broil for an additional 2-3 minutes to brown the top.

Step 7: Serve the baked salmon with extra lemon wedges on the side. Enjoy!

Helpful Tips:
1. Preheat the oven to 400°F and line a baking sheet with parchment paper

2. Place the salmon fillets on the prepared baking sheet and season with salt and pepper.

3. Mix together chopped fresh dill, minced garlic, lemon juice, and olive oil in a small bowl.

4. Spread the dill mixture evenly over the salmon fillets.

5. Top the salmon with lemon slices for added flavor.

6. Bake in the preheated oven for 12-15 minutes, or until the salmon is cooked through.

7. Serve the baked salmon hot, garnished with additional dill and lemon wedges. Enjoy!

Lentil soup with vegetables

Ingredients:

- 1 cup of green or brown lentils
- 4 cups of vegetable broth
- 1 onion, chopped
- 2 carrots, diced
- 2 celery stalks, chopped
- 1 can of diced tomatoes
- 2 cloves of garlic, minced
- Salt and pepper to taste

Equipment:

1. Pot
2. Ladle
3. Knife
4. Cutting board
5. Spoon
6. Stockpot

Methods:

Step 1: Rinse 1 cup of lentils under cold water and set aside.

Step 2: In a large pot, heat 1 tablespoon of olive oil over medium heat.

Step 3: Add 1 diced onion, 2 minced garlic cloves, 2 diced carrots, and 2 diced celery stalks to the pot and cook until softened.

Step 4: Stir in 1 teaspoon of cumin, 1 teaspoon of paprika, and salt and pepper to taste.

Step 5: Add the rinsed lentils, 6 cups of vegetable broth, and 1 can of diced tomatoes to the pot.

Step 6: Simmer for 30-45 minutes until the lentils are tender.

Step 7: Serve hot and garnish with fresh parsley.

Helpful Tips:

1. Start by sautéing onions, carrots, and celery as a flavorful base for your lentil soup.

2. Use a variety of vegetables such as tomatoes, bell peppers, and spinach to add depth and nutrients.

3. Consider adding herbs and spices like cumin, paprika, and thyme for extra flavor.

4. Rinse and drain your lentils before adding them to the pot to remove any excess starch.

5. Use vegetable broth or stock instead of water for a richer taste.

6. Let the soup simmer on low heat for at least 30 minutes to allow the flavors to meld together.

7. Season with salt and pepper to taste before serving. Enjoy your hearty and nutritious lentil soup!

Brown rice stir-fry with tofu and vegetables

Ingredients:
- 1 cup of brown rice
- 1 block of tofu
- 2 cups of mixed vegetables
- Soy sauce, garlic, and ginger
- cooking oil

Equipment:
1. Wok
2. Spatula
3. Cutting board
4. Knife
5. Mixing bowl

Methods:

Step 1: Cook 1 cup of brown rice according to package instructions.

Step 2: Press tofu to remove excess water, then cut into cubes.

Step 3: Heat oil in a large skillet over medium heat.

Step 4: Add tofu cubes and cook until browned on all sides.

Step 5: Remove tofu from skillet and set aside.

Step 6: In the same skillet, add chopped vegetables (such as bell peppers, broccoli, and carrots) and sauté until tender.

Step 7: Add cooked brown rice and tofu back to the skillet.

Step 8: Drizzle with soy sauce and stir to combine.

Step 9: Cook for an additional 2-3 minutes.

Step 10: Serve hot and enjoy your brown rice stir-fry with tofu and vegetables!

Helpful Tips:

1. Start by cooking brown rice according to package instructions.

2. Press tofu to remove excess water and cut into cubes.

3. Heat a pan with oil and stir-fry tofu until golden brown.

4. Add chopped vegetables (bell peppers, broccoli, carrots, etc.) to the pan.

5. Season with soy sauce, minced garlic, ginger, and a pinch of red pepper flakes.

6. Cook until the vegetables are tender but still slightly crisp.

7. Add cooked brown rice to the pan and mix well.

8. Serve hot and garnish with sesame seeds and green onions. Enjoy your nutritious brown rice stir-fry with tofu and vegetables!

Steamed shrimp with cocktail sauce

Ingredients:
- 1 lb medium shrimp
- 1/4 cup ketchup
- 1 tbsp horseradish
- 1 tsp lemon juice
- Salt to taste

Equipment:
1. Pot
2. Strainer
3. Mixing bowl
4. Whisk
5. Tongs

Methods:
Step 1: Peel and devein shrimp, leaving tails intact.

Step 2: Season shrimp with salt and pepper.

Step 3: Fill a pot with 2 inches of water and bring to a boil.

Step 4: Place a steamer basket in the pot and add shrimp in a single layer.

Step 5: Cover and steam shrimp for 3-4 minutes or until pink and cooked through.

Step 6: In a small bowl, mix together ketchup, horseradish, Worcestershire sauce, lemon juice, and hot sauce to make cocktail sauce.

Step 7: Serve steamed shrimp with cocktail sauce on the side for dipping.

Step 8: Enjoy your delicious steamed shrimp appetizer!

Helpful Tips:
1. Start by choosing fresh shrimp and removing the shells and tails before steaming.

2. Season the shrimp with salt, pepper, and a squeeze of lemon juice for added flavor.

3. Place a steamer basket in a pot with a small amount of water at the bottom to steam the shrimp.

4. Steam the shrimp for 4-6 minutes or until they turn pink and opaque.

5. While the shrimp is steaming, mix together ketchup, horseradish, Worcestershire sauce, and lemon juice to make a tangy cocktail sauce.

6. Serve the steamed shrimp with the homemade cocktail sauce for a delicious appetizer or meal.

Turkey and avocado wrap

Ingredients:
- 1 lb. cooked turkey breast, sliced
- 2 ripe avocados, sliced
- 4 whole wheat wraps
- 1 cup shredded lettuce

Equipment:
1. Knife
2. Cutting board
3. Frying pan
4. Spatula
5. Mixing bowl

Methods:
Step 1: Start by cooking the turkey breast in a skillet over medium heat until fully cooked.

Step 2: Once the turkey is cooked, slice it into thin pieces.

Step 3: Mash the avocado in a bowl and season with salt and pepper to taste.

Step 4: Lay out a large tortilla and spread the mashed avocado evenly over the surface.

Step 5: Place the sliced turkey on top of the avocado.

Step 6: Add any desired toppings such as lettuce, tomato, cheese, or salsa.

Step 7: Roll up the tortilla tightly, tucking in the ends as you go.

Step 8: Slice the wrap in half and enjoy!

Helpful Tips:
1. Start with fresh ingredients - choose ripe avocados and high-quality turkey.

2. Season the turkey with your favorite spices for added flavor.

3. Heat up the wrap on a skillet or in the microwave for a few seconds to make it more pliable.

4. Layer the turkey and avocado on the wrap, leaving room around the edges for easy rolling.

5. Add any additional toppings such as lettuce, tomato, or cheese for extra flavor.

6. Roll up the wrap tightly, tucking in the sides as you go.

7. Cut the wrap in half for easy eating and enjoy your delicious Turkey and Avocado Wrap!

Lemon herb roasted turkey breast

Ingredients:
- 2 pounds turkey breast
- 1 lemon
- 2 cloves garlic
- 1 tablespoon olive oil
- Salt and pepper to taste
- Fresh herbs (thyme, rosemary, parsley)

Equipment:
1. Roasting pan
2. Basting brush
3. Meat thermometer
4. Oven mitts
5. Carving knife

Methods:
Step 1: Preheat the oven to 350°F.

Step 2: In a small bowl, mix together 1/4 cup of olive oil, 2 tablespoons of freshly squeezed lemon juice, 1 tablespoon of minced garlic, 1 tablespoon of chopped fresh parsley, 1 teaspoon of dried oregano, 1 teaspoon of dried thyme, and salt and pepper to taste.

Step 3: Place a 2-3 pound turkey breast in a roasting pan.

Step 4: Rub the herb mixture all over the turkey breast.

Step 5: Roast the turkey breast in the preheated oven for 1-1.5 hours, or until the internal temperature reaches 165°F.

Step 6: Let the turkey breast rest for 10 minutes before slicing and serving.

Helpful Tips:
1. Preheat your oven to 350°F.

2. Mix together a marinade of olive oil, lemon juice, garlic, and herbs such as rosemary, thyme, and oregano.

3. Rub the marinade all over the turkey breast, ensuring it is evenly coated.

4. Place the turkey breast in a roasting pan and cover with foil.

5. Roast for approximately 1.5 to 2 hours, or until the internal temperature reaches 165°F.

6. Allow the turkey breast to rest for at least 10 minutes before slicing and serving.

7. Garnish with fresh herbs and lemon slices for a beautiful presentation.

Turkey and vegetable kabobs

Ingredients:

- 1 lb turkey breast, cubed
- 2 zucchinis, cut into chunks
- 1 red bell pepper, cut into chunks
- 1 red onion, cut into chunks

Equipment:

1. Skewers
2. Grill pan
3. Tongs
4. Knife
5. Cutting board

Methods:

Step 1: Soak wooden skewers in water for at least 30 minutes.

Step 2: Preheat grill to medium-high heat.

Step 3: Cut turkey breast into bite-sized pieces and place in a bowl.

Step 4: Mix olive oil, lemon juice, minced garlic, and chopped fresh herb in a separate bowl.

Step 5: Pour marinade over turkey pieces and let marinate for 30 minutes.

Step 6: Cut vegetables (such as bell peppers, zucchini, and red onion) into bite-sized pieces and thread onto skewers with marinated turkey.

Step 7: Grill kabobs for 10-12 minutes, turning occasionally, until turkey is cooked through and vegetables are tender.

Step 8: Serve hot and enjoy!

Helpful Tips:

1. Soak wooden skewers in water for at least 30 minutes before using to prevent them from burning.

2. Use a variety of colorful vegetables, such as bell peppers, zucchini, red onions, and cherry tomatoes, to make your kabobs visually appealing.

3. Marinate the turkey pieces in a mixture of olive oil, lemon juice, garlic and herbs for at least 30 minutes to add extra flavor.

4. Alternate threading the turkey and vegetables onto the skewers to ensure even cooking.

5. Cook the kabobs on a preheated grill or in the oven, turning occasionally until the turkey is cooked through and the vegetables are tender.

6. Serve with a side of rice or a salad for a complete meal.

Baked tilapia with garlic and herb seasoning

Ingredients:
- 4 tilapia fillets
- 4 cloves of garlic, minced
- 2 tsp dried parsley
- 1 tsp dried thyme
- 1 tsp dried oregano
- Salt and pepper to taste

Equipment:
1. Baking dish
2. Mixing bowl
3. Whisk
4. Spatula
5. Cooking spray
6. Oven mitts

Methods:
Step 1: Preheat the oven to 400°F (200°C).

Step 2: Rinse the tilapia fillets with cold water and pat them dry with paper towels.

Step 3: In a small bowl, mix together minced garlic, dried herbs (such as basil, thyme, and parsley), salt, pepper, and olive oil to create a seasoning paste.

Step 4: Place the tilapia fillets on a baking sheet lined with parchment paper.

Step 5: Spread the seasoning paste evenly over the top of each fillet.

Step 6: Bake in the preheated oven for 12-15 minutes, or until the fish flakes easily with a fork.

Step 7: Serve hot and enjoy your delicious baked tilapia with garlic and herb seasoning!

Helpful Tips:
1. Preheat your oven to 400°F.

2. Rinse the tilapia fillets under cold water and pat them dry with paper towels.

3. Season the fillets with salt, pepper, garlic powder, onion powder, and dried herbs such as oregano, thyme, and basil.

4. Drizzle olive oil over the fillets and rub the seasoning into the fish.

5. Place the fillets on a baking sheet lined with parchment paper.

6. Bake in the preheated oven for 10-12 minutes or until the fish is flaky and opaque.

7. Serve hot with a squeeze of lemon juice and fresh herbs for garnish.

8. Enjoy your delicious and healthy meal!

Roasted vegetable salad with balsamic vinaigrette

Ingredients:

- Assorted vegetables (bell peppers, zucchini, red onions)
- Olive oil
- Balsamic vinegar
- Honey
- Dijon mustard
- Salt and pepper

(Note: Quantities will vary based on personal preference and availability of ingredients)

Equipment:

1. Baking sheet
2. Mixing bowl
3. Whisk
4. Chef's knife
5. Salad tongs

Methods:

Step 1: Preheat the oven to 400°F.

Step 2: Cut your choice of vegetables (such as bell peppers, zucchini, cherry tomatoes) into bite-sized pieces.

Step 3: Toss the vegetables in olive oil, salt, and pepper.

Step 4: Spread the vegetables in a single layer on a baking sheet.

Step 5: Roast the vegetables in the oven for 20-25 minutes, or until they are tender and slightly browned.

Step 6: In a small bowl, whisk together balsamic vinegar, olive oil, Dijon mustard, honey, and salt.

Step 7: Drizzle the vinaigrette over the roasted vegetables before serving. Enjoy your delicious roasted vegetable salad!

Helpful Tips:

1. Preheat your oven to 400°F before you begin prepping your vegetables.

2. Cut your vegetables into similar-sized pieces to ensure even roasting.

3. Toss your vegetables in olive oil, salt, and pepper before placing them on baking sheet.

4. Roast your vegetables for about 20-25 minutes, or until they are tender and slightly caramelized.

5. While your vegetables are roasting, prepare your balsamic vinaigrette by whisking together balsamic vinegar, olive oil, Dijon mustard, honey, and salt.

6. Once your vegetables are done roasting, let them cool slightly before ossing them with the balsamic vinaigrette.

7. Serve your roasted vegetable salad warm or at room temperature for the best flavor.

Grilled shrimp skewers with mango salsa

Ingredients:
- 1 lb shrimp
- 1 mango
- 1 red bell pepper
- 1 shallot
- 1 lime
- 2 tbsp olive oil
- Salt and pepper to taste

Equipment:
1. Grill
2. Skewers
3. Cutting board
4. Knife
5. Mixing bowl
6. Sauté pan

Methods:
Step 1: Preheat grill to medium-high heat.

Step 2: Peel and devein shrimp, leaving tails on.

Step 3: Thread shrimp onto skewers, alternating with pieces of bell pepper and onion.

Step 4: In a bowl, combine diced mango, red onion, jalapeno, lime juice and cilantro to make salsa.

Step 5: Brush shrimp skewers with olive oil and season with salt and pepper

Step 6: Grill skewers for 2-3 minutes per side, until shrimp are pink and opaque.

Step 7: Serve shrimp skewers with mango salsa on the side. Enjoy!

Helpful Tips:
1. Soak skewers in water for at least 30 minutes to prevent them from burning on the grill.

2. Preheat the grill to medium-high heat and oil the grates to prevent sticking.

3. Season the shrimp with salt, pepper, and your favorite seasoning before skewering.

4. Grill the shrimp skewers for 2-3 minutes per side or until they are pink and opaque.

5. To make the mango salsa, combine diced mango, red onion, cilantro, lime juice, and salt in a bowl.

6. Allow the salsa to sit for at least 30 minutes before serving to let the flavors meld together.

7. Serve the grilled shrimp skewers with the mango salsa on top for a delicious and refreshing dish.

Lemon garlic chicken skewers

Ingredients:

- 1 lb of chicken breast
- 2 cloves of garlic
- 1 lemon
- 2 tbsp of olive oil
- Salt and pepper
- Wooden skewers

Equipment:

1. Skewers
2. Mixing bowl
3. Whisk
4. Grill pan
5. Tongs

Methods:

Step 1: In a small bowl, combine lemon juice, minced garlic, olive oil, salt, and pepper to make the marinade.

Step 2: Cut boneless, skinless chicken breasts into bite-sized pieces.

Step 3: Place the chicken pieces in a zip-top bag and pour the marinade over them. Seal the bag and refrigerate for at least 30 minutes.

Step 4: Preheat a grill or grill pan over medium-high heat.

Step 5: Thread the marinated chicken pieces onto skewers.

Step 6: Grill the skewers for about 5-6 minutes per side, or until the chicken is cooked through.

Step 7: Serve the lemon garlic chicken skewers hot and enjoy!

Helpful Tips:

1. Marinate the chicken in lemon juice, garlic, olive oil, salt, and pepper for at least 30 minutes before skewering.

2. Alternate the chicken pieces with slices of lemon on the skewers for extra flavor.

3. Preheat the grill to medium-high heat before adding the skewers.

4. Cook the skewers for about 10-12 minutes, turning occasionally, until the chicken is cooked through.

5. Serve the skewers with a side of rice or salad for a complete meal.

6. Garnish with freshly chopped parsley or lemon zest for added freshness.

7. Don't forget to soak wooden skewers in water for at least 30 minutes before using to prevent burning.